Liberty and Learning

Liberty and Learning

Academic Freedom for Teachers and Students

David Moshman

Foreword by ReLeah Cossett Lent

HEINEMANN
Portsmouth, NH

Heinemann
361 Hanover Street
Portsmouth, NH 03801–3912
www.heinemann.com

Offices and agents throughout the world

Library of Congress Cataloging-in-Publication Data
Moshman, David.
    Liberty and learning : academic freedom for teachers and students / David Moshman.
        p. cm.
    Includes bibliographical references and index.
    ISBN-13: 978-0-325-02121-8
    ISBN-10: 0-325-02121-X
1. Academic freedom—United States. I. Title.
    LC72.2.M67 2009
    371.1'04—dc22   2009012591

Editor: James Strickland
Production editor: Sonja S. Chapman
Typesetter: Publishers' Design and Production Services, Inc.
Cover design: Night & Day Design
Manufacturing: Valerie Cooper

Printed in the United States of America on acid-free paper
13 12 11 10 09   PAH   1 2 3 4 5

Contents

Foreword by ReLeah Cossett Lent vii

Preface xi

PART ONE   Liberty, Learning, and Academic Freedom   1

Chapter 1   **With Liberty for Whom?   3**
Institutional Autonomy   4
Faculty Autonomy   5
Student Rights   6
Parental Authority   8
Education By and For the Community   9
Conclusion: Academic Freedom as Intellectual
    Freedom   11
A Legal Interlude   13

Chapter 2   **The Constitutionalization of Academic Freedom   15**
West Virginia v. Barnette: Freedom from
    Indoctrination   16
Keyishian v. Board of Regents: Intellectual Freedom
    in Education   22

Chapter 3   **From Armbands to Bong Hits in the
U.S. Supreme Court   30**
Tinker v. Des Moines: Freedom of Expression   30
Hazelwood v. Kuhlmeier: School Authority over
    Curriculum   32
Morse v. Frederick: Bong Hits 4 Jesus   40
Conclusion   42

Chapter 4   **Principles of Academic Freedom   46**
1. Freedom of Belief and Identity   47
2. Freedom of Expression and Discussion   48
3. Freedom of Inquiry   50
4. Freedom from Indoctrination   51
5. Equality, Privacy, and Due Process   54
Conclusion   55

PART TWO   Academic Freedom in Practice   57

Chapter 5   **Canon to the Right of Us, Canon to the Left:
Literature, Selection, and Censorship   59**

Chapter 6   **Apes and Evolutionists: Biology and Ideology   72**

Chapter 7   **"Don't Know Much About History": Genocide, Denial,
and Indoctrination   86**

Chapter 8   **Tolerating the Intolerant: Bad Words and Worse   98**

Chapter 9   **The Birds, the Bees, and the Censors: Sex Education
and Its Discontents   108**

Chapter 10   **Doing Right and Being Good: Morality, Values,
and Character   120**

Chapter 11   **Ultimate Questions: Religion and Beyond   132**

Appendix   **Principles of Academic Freedom   143**

Book Study   145

References and Suggested Readings   147

Index   155

Foreword

I know censorship, and it is through the lens of such intimate encounters that I read this remarkable book. If only I had been able to access David Moshman's wisdom during the years when I was struggling to explain the importance of academic freedom to parents, administrators, and school board members who sought to restrict such freedom from my students. My staunch commitment to resisting censorship in any form made it incongruous to me that others could hold an opposing view with equal fervor. I couldn't come to grips with such a reality, although I can now acknowledge that I didn't fully understand the underlying complexities of academic freedom. While I argued with conviction that such freedoms were the most fundamental tenets of education, I could not adequately define them, offer compelling examples, or speak without such strong emotion that it threatened to sabotage my position. I knew that learners must be afforded the freedom to try on their own beliefs, entertain ideas that may be foreign, even abhorrent, to them, and push beyond the conventional wisdom espoused in sanitized textbooks if they were to brush against truth, but knowing what I believed was simply not enough. Perhaps the rather naïve understanding with which I approached these issues is where many educators find themselves today. They know *about* academic freedom, they understand that it is essential to learning and to our continuing democracy, but the absolutes elude them.

David Moshman, in a grand understatement, tells us that the ideas in this book were not "sketched on a napkin" a few days before publication. If anything is clear from the first page of *Liberty and Learning*, it is that David has spent many years immersed in all facets of academic freedom, a concept that seems to have confounded some of the brightest minds in the last century. The first three chapters could stand alone as a gripping and often disturbing history of academic freedom as they demonstrate how the seemingly airtight First Amendment is subject to surprising interpretations. David's concise, accessible analysis of pertinent cases, along with important quotes from majority and minority opinions, provides a deep understanding of how academic freedom has come to have minimum protection under the First Amendment. Despite our concerns about such interpretations, it is important to be armed with this knowledge, even as we remain committed to reversing the trend.

It is the scenarios in the last half of the book, however, that will grab you—and won't let go. The "what-ifs," many based on actual situations from David's work with intellectual freedom groups, create an interactive reading experience that may make you sweat, especially when they end with the challenge: "You are the teacher." Some of the situations may strike too close to home for comfort as you recall students, situations, texts, or comments that could turn up in similar scenarios. This brilliant approach is exactly the manner in which such topics should be addressed, through pointed discussions that allow for a slow settling in of understanding, even while wrestling with the questions.

And then, there are Moshman's five principles of academic freedom, principles that I predict will become infused in the daily workings of classrooms and districts across the country. I strongly encourage teachers, administrators, districts, and state boards of education to call a hiatus to their testing, curriculum planning, and ubiquitous staff meetings to make time to read this book together. Now, perhaps more than at any time in our past, our children are facing environmental, political, and financial challenges that we could scarcely have imagined even a decade ago. Students must be given opportunities to come to know what they believe and expand their thinking through self-reflection and deliberation within safe classroom environments. Above all, we must ensure that we do not, as Justice Jackson said more than sixty years ago, "strangle the free mind at its source and teach youth to discount important principles of our government as mere platitudes"(43). I would argue that it is nearly impossible to release the free mind without understanding the complex nature of academic freedom and untangling its complexities in an effort to promote clear and cogent thinking. Perhaps I had such difficulty expressing what I knew to be true during my battles against censorship because I had not experienced opportunities in my own education to explore the nuances of academic freedom.

If my challengers could have read *Liberty and Learning*, they may well have understood that it is not only our collective obligation but our privilege to guard the academic rights of our students and their teachers. Such rights, as defined by Moshman's principles of academic freedom, include the rights of students and teachers to "believe and value whatever they believe and value ... to express their views and to discuss them with others ... and [ ] to pursue their own interests and ideas" (143). Furthermore, we must not require or coerce students to modify their beliefs or values and must guarantee that all students and faculty have equal rights to privacy and due process (144). Imagine a community coming together to discuss these principles as seriously and intentionally as they do other issues of far less importance.

No matter how you choose to use this book—as a catalyst for group dialogue, a prompt for contemplation, or a vehicle for community action, its ideas will advance the current notions of education in immeasurable ways. David Moshman's flawless research, probing questions, and insightful principles will lay the foundation for a new era in academic freedom, perhaps prompting school systems to create strong policies to guard against censorship and other challenges to intellectual freedom. And our mantra for the future? As David so concisely writes, "Learning without liberty is indoctrination, not education." *Liberty and Learning* is the perfect place to continue our own academic freedom education. Read this important book and join the conversation.

—ReLeah Cossett Lent

Preface

Consider the following cases (numbered as they appear in Chapters 5–11):

Case 5–2 *You are a student in a literature course in which most of the assigned novels are written by women or by men of non-European background. You wonder if some of these novels were included in the course not because of their intrinsic value but because of the demographic characteristics of their authors. You feel like you're being indoctrinated in multiculturalism and diversity but you expect that your instructor and most of your fellow students will deem you racist or sexist if you question the selection of novels. What should you do?*

Case 7–1 *As a history teacher covering a unit on World War II, you discuss the Holocaust, which you define as the Nazi effort to exterminate Jews and Gypsies. A student suggests that the Nazi campaign against Gypsies was not genocidal and thus not part of the Holocaust. Another student argues, to the contrary, that not only did the Nazis commit genocide against Jews and Gypsies but the Holocaust also included exterminations of Poles, homosexuals, Jehovah's Witnesses, the disabled, and others. A third student responds that many people from many backgrounds died in World War II but there was no specific Nazi effort to exterminate particular groups. A fourth student adds that the Holocaust is a myth devised by Jews to create support for the state of Israel. A fifth student denounces the fourth as anti-Semitic and demands an apology or appropriate punishment. What should you do?*

Case 8–3 *In a discussion of human rights, a student argues that fundamental rights include the right not to be discriminated against because of your sexual orientation. Another student says this sort of absurd claim shows the problem with vague notions of human rights. A third student agrees with the second, noting how vagueness leads to overly broad conceptions of rights that protect immoral behavior and evil people. A fourth student adds that human rights can't protect everyone and everything. The first student replies that human rights are, by definition, rights that protect all people. "Yeah, people," murmurs a fifth student, "not faggots." You're the teacher.*

Case 10–2 *As a teacher committed to academic freedom you don't want to force your own values on your students, but you also don't want to neglect the realm of values. Your solution is to present your students with dilemmas that pit competing values against each other and to ask them to identify, articulate, and prioritize their own values in the course of discussing these dilemmas. You consistently urge students to respect each other's views and values, as you do. Students report home that you think everyone is entitled to his or her own values, leading to parental complaints that you are teaching moral relativism. How should you respond?*

Case 11–7 *Your school has a long-standing tradition that the senior with the best academic record delivers a valedictory address at graduation. This year's valedictorian lets it be known that she is planning to thank Jesus for helping her get through school and will ask the audience to join her in prayer. As the responsible administrator, what should you do?*

Schools, colleges, universities, and educational systems all over the world routinely face disputes about what students should see, hear, read, and do. How shall we decide what topics to teach and what facts, concepts, ideas, and viewpoints to present? Who should decide what research students and faculty pursue and what conclusions they reach? Should history be presented and studied objectively? Patriotically? As a moral lesson? All of the above? What about sexuality? What about religion? Should we promote values? Morality? Responsibility? Student development? How may we do this? Should we use schools as a means of cultural transformation? Toward what ends?

Who should have the authority to make these sorts of decisions? And what about academic freedom?

Two conceptions have long dominated discussion of academic freedom in the United States. One, which emerged in the early part of the twentieth century, is the American Association of University Professors' conception of academic freedom as faculty autonomy and authority in higher education. The other, which emerged in the middle portion of the twentieth century but has been on the decline since the 1980s, is the constitutional conception of academic freedom as a First Amendment right of individual students and faculty in public educational institutions. These traditional conceptions, and others, are reviewed in the first three chapters.

Chapter 4 presents an integrative vision of academic freedom as intellectual freedom in educational and research contexts. Rather than a special privilege of college faculty or a legal right of individuals, academic freedom is an intrinsic condition for teaching, learning, and inquiry at all levels of education. Five principles of academic freedom—encompassing freedoms of belief, expression, and inquiry—are presented, explained, and justified. The principles are then applied, in Chapters 5 through 11, to diverse cases and controversies spanning literature, science, history, tolerance, sexuality, morality, and religion. Most of these cases are seen through the eyes of teachers or students, but some take the perspective of parents, administrators, governing board members, or legislators.

The five principles were not generated on a rigorous schedule of one principle per hour, week, or year, nor were they sketched on a party napkin two days before the manuscript for this book was due to the publisher. They began with my efforts over the course of the 1980s to develop a set of principles concerning the intellectual and First Amendment rights of children and adolescents in educational contexts, a direct outgrowth of my work as a developmental and cognitive psychologist with a particular interest in education. I have also been active since the early 1980s in the Nebraska affiliate of the American Civil Liberties Union (ACLU), especially with regard to the First Amendment rights of children, students, parents, and teachers, and in the University of Nebraska–Lincoln (UNL) chapter of the American Association of University Professors (AAUP), especially with regard to matters of academic freedom. These various concerns came together in a set of principles of academic freedom I developed for the Academic Freedom Coalition of Nebraska (AFCON), which adopted them in 1999. The present principles (discussed in Chapter 4 and collected in the Appendix) are an expanded version of the AFCON principles.

The cases that make up the final seven chapters of the book are presented as brief hypothetical vignettes, but they are based on hundreds of actual cases that have come to my attention over the past three decades, often in connection with ACLU Nebraska, the UNL AAUP, or AFCON. Within AFCON, in particular, I have had the opportunity to work with teachers and students on academic freedom controversies of all sorts at all levels of education. In an age where everyone demands more control of teachers, students, curriculum, and instruction, and ever-increasing assessment and accountability, these collaborations have reaffirmed my conviction that what education really needs, above all, is more intellectual freedom. With that in mind, I dedicate this book to the Academic Freedom Coalition of Nebraska, and to academic freedom activists everywhere.

Part One

Liberty, Learning, and Academic Freedom

Chapter 1
With Liberty for Whom?

What is academic freedom? For many centuries, academic freedom has been construed as the autonomy of educational institutions with regard to external political, religious, and ideological pressures. When government or church acts to restrict teaching or research with regard to some topic or viewpoint, it is acting contrary to norms of academic freedom.

Academic freedom is also the autonomy of faculty—teachers and researchers, individually and collectively—at least with regard to curriculum and research. If an administrator, governing board, or legislature deletes ideas from the curriculum or forbids research on specific topics, faculty may justly claim that this is an infringement on their academic freedom. Similarly, the collective faculty intrudes on the academic freedom of individual faculty when it uses its authority over curriculum to restrict their intellectual freedom.

Academic freedom can also be seen as a moral or legal right of students to be educated rather than indoctrinated. Restrictions on belief, expression, discussion, and inquiry violate the intellectual freedom of students regardless of whether these restrictions are imposed by teachers, administrators, governing boards, or legislatures. In the case of minors, moreover, parents have authority with regard to the education of their own children.

Finally, there is the community that institutes the educational system. What interests or rights does this community have, and how are these related to academic freedom?

Academic freedom, then, has been construed to mean (a) the freedom of educational institutions from external control; (b) the freedom of faculty from institutional and external control, especially with regard to curriculum and research; and (c) the freedom of students to formulate, express, and discuss their own views. It is also closely associated with (d) the freedom of parents to direct the education of their minor children and (e) the freedom of a community to educate the next generation in accord with its beliefs and values. In this chapter I discuss each of these five freedoms and their intricate interrelations. I conclude that academic freedom is best construed as intellectual freedom in educational and research contexts.

Institutional Autonomy

For many centuries, academic freedom referred primarily to the freedom of universities from governmental and ecclesiastical control. This conception of academic freedom as the autonomy of universities may be considered the historical meaning of the concept, and remains one of its core meanings. External efforts to control universities raise questions of academic freedom.

Why should universities be autonomous? The standard argument is simple and convincing: research and teaching require intellectual freedom. Thus educational institutions must be insulated from external ideological pressures.

Although the concept of academic freedom arose largely in the context of higher education, learning and development require intellectual freedom at all ages. Children and adolescents actively construct increasingly complex structures of knowledge and increasingly powerful modes of thinking and reasoning in environments that encourage them to seek and question information, formulate their own ideas, and engage in open discussion. Intellectual freedom, then, is foundational at all levels of education. Academic freedom can be taken to refer to the autonomy of educational institutions at elementary, secondary, and higher levels—at least when such autonomy is intended to promote intellectual freedom within the institution.

A democracy that sponsors a system of public education faces the special problem that government cannot fail to exercise some degree of control over a government-sponsored educational system. At the same time, institutional autonomy is a critical constraint on governmental indoctrination. A democratic system of public education must not undermine democracy by acting contrary to the will of the people but also must not undermine democracy by indoctrinating students in particular political, religious, or other doctrines—even if these doctrines have majority support. Democratic education raises particularly complex and subtle issues regarding the relation of the government to education.

To say an institution is autonomous leaves open questions about who makes decisions on behalf of the institution, and on what basis. Thus we must consider the internal structure of academic governance, including the role of faculty in academic decisions.

Faculty Autonomy

Institutional autonomy is intended to protect intellectual freedom. At the very least, this includes assuring that curriculum and research are designed and pursued on the basis of academic considerations. Administrators and governing boards, however, have no special expertise with regard to curriculum, instruction, or inquiry in the diverse fields that faculty represent. On the contrary, at all levels of education, it is the faculty who are hired on the basis of their academic expertise. Governing boards and administrators, moreover, are beholden to the agendas of those who elect or appoint them, whereas faculty can be more readily protected, through a tenure system, from political constraints on their academic decisions. If the purpose of institutional autonomy is to protect intellectual freedom, it is faculty, above all, who should exercise that autonomy. In the words of the American Association of University Professors' 1940 Statement of Principles, "teachers are entitled to full freedom in research and in the publication of the results ... [and] to freedom in the classroom in discussing their subject."

Faculty authority over curriculum and research is best construed as a responsibility, not a right. Operating both collectively and individually, faculty must formulate and implement plans for teaching and inquiry that are academically defensible, not driven by political or other external pressures. They must have the freedom to do this because without such freedom they cannot teach and conduct research in a manner consistent with their professional expertise and obligations. As surely as a carpenter needs a hammer or a cellist needs a cello, teachers and researchers need academic freedom to do what they are supposed to do.

The academic freedom of faculty, then, may be seen as resting, in part, on the right of faculty as employees to job conditions that enable them to do their jobs. But this is a general right of employees, not a special right of faculty. Faculty autonomy thus rests not on a right peculiar to faculty but on the expectation that autonomy will enable faculty to provide the best education, conduct the best research, and protect their students from indoctrination.

With regard to public education, it might be thought that insulation of academic decision making from the political process is undemocratic. Shouldn't the public decide what is taught in their schools? And doesn't that mean the majority rules?

But restrictions on popular control are not inherently antidemocratic. We expect the medical operations of a public hospital to be directed by physicians and other medical professionals. We expect legal cases to be resolved by judges, or by jurors acting under their direction. Similarly, it is fully consistent with democracy to expect the curriculum of public schools to be determined by those with relevant expertise, not by a vote of the general public. A strong case can be made, in fact, that the democratic legitimacy of public education derives from the possibility of delegating curricular authority to faculty and insulating them from political pressures.

Faculty autonomy refers both to the collective authority of the faculty and to the freedom of individual teachers and researchers. Thus it includes both (a) the authority of academic departments, curriculum committees, and faculty senates and (b) the freedom of individual faculty to teach and conduct research in accord with their academic judgments. To construe academic freedom as faculty autonomy leaves open the question of to what extent the collective faculty may dictate curricular content and research agendas and to what extent individual faculty should be free to make such decisions with regard to their own classes or research programs.

As a matter of political reality, elementary and secondary school faculty, both individually and collectively, usually have less autonomy than their counterparts in higher education. There is no convincing basis for this distinction, however. Faculty autonomy is essential at all levels of education.

Student Rights

Intellectual freedom fosters learning and development and thus serves the purposes of education. With respect to students, however, intellectual freedom is not simply a means to a pedagogical end. Respect for students entails respect for their rights as developing rational agents to formulate, express, and discuss their own views. Educational institutions may present specific ideas and values, but they must not punish expression of, or restrict access to, alternative ideas and values.

Students, in other words, have both an educational interest in intellectual freedom and a moral right to it. Intellectual freedom is in students' best *interest* because it promotes learning and development. It is also a *right* of each individual student because the alternative—indoctrination—fails to respect students as persons. The right of students to intellectual freedom is, at its academic core, a right not to be indoctrinated.

What does it mean to be indoctrinated? To be indoctrinated is to have your beliefs manipulated and shaped via externally directed processes without due regard for your present and future autonomy. In prototypical cases, this is done systematically with the intent that you will internalize and maintain specific political, religious, or other doctrines. In other cases the indoctrinative processes may be less deliberate and systematic, but nevertheless distinct from rational teaching and learning.

What's wrong with indoctrination? It violates the right of students to formulate their own beliefs and values, especially their most fundamental identity commitments, and to operate autonomously in the future. In extreme cases, indoctrination treats students simply as means to the end of furthering the doctrines of those who formulate the curriculum. Widespread and systematic indoctrination, moreover, not only violates the rights of individual students but arguably violates the collective right of an entire generation to forge its own beliefs and values.

Faculty have long recognized that their academic freedom entails a corresponding responsibility to respect the academic freedom of their students. In the United States, the Code of Ethics of the Education Profession, adopted by the 1975 representative assembly of the National Education Association, highlights the ethical responsibility of educators to protect what it calls the "freedom to learn":

> The educator strives to help each student realize his or her potential as a worthy and effective member of society. The educator therefore works to stimulate the spirit of inquiry, the acquisition of knowledge and understanding, and the thoughtful formulation of worthy goals.
>
> In fulfillment of the obligation to the student, the educator
>
> 1. Shall not unreasonably restrain the student from independent action in the pursuit of learning.

2. Shall not unreasonably deny the student access to varying points of view.
3. Shall not deliberately suppress or distort subject matter relevant to the student's progress.

Similarly, the 1987 Statement on Professional Ethics of the American Association of University Professors (AAUP) specifies that "as teachers, professors encourage the free pursuit of learning in their students. . . . They protect their academic freedom." The AAUP's 1966 Statement on Government of Colleges and Universities specifies that students should have the opportunity "to be listened to in the classroom without fear of institutional reprisal for the substance of their views." The 1967 Joint Statement on Rights and Freedoms of Students—endorsed by the AAUP, the U.S. National Student Association, the Association of American Colleges, and other organizations—declared "Freedom to teach and freedom to learn are inseparable facets of academic freedom."

> The professor in the classroom and in conference should encourage free discussion, inquiry, and expression. Student performance should be evaluated solely on an academic basis, not on opinions or conduct in matters unrelated to academic standards. . . . Students should be free to take reasoned exception to the data or views offered in any course of study and to reserve judgment about matters of opinion, but they are responsible for learning the content of any course of study for which they are enrolled.

To say students have a right not to be indoctrinated is not to say that teachers and educational institutions may not present them with ideas and try to convince them to change their views. Nonindoctrination requires, however, that efforts to persuade take place in a context of intellectual freedom, in which students are free (and know they are) to have ideas of their own; to express and discuss these ideas; to seek out additional information and ideas; and to construct their own beliefs, values, doctrines, and identities.

Parental Authority

I have been speaking of students in general, addressing issues fully pertinent at all levels of education. When the students are children, their rights may be exercised at least in part by their parents or other guardians. Given that children may be less able than adults to recognize and protect themselves against indoctrination, parents have a responsibility to protect their children's intellectual freedom and future autonomy. Thus parents have important interests and responsibilities with regard to their children's education.

Because parents are generally at least as likely as anyone to act in the interests of their children, respect for parental authority typically serves to protect the rights of children. Especially for very young children, parental authority and children's rights may be construed together as part of family autonomy. Even for children of elementary school age, the best way to protect the rights of individual students is usually to acknowledge and respect parental choices as family decisions.

Parent and child interests do not always coincide, however, and children have rights of their own. Parents may act on the basis of motives unrelated or even antithetical to the welfare of their children. They may ignore or undermine their children's interests and rights with regard to education. Thus parental authority cannot be absolute.

Older children and adolescents, moreover, may be fully capable of determining and furthering their own interests and exercising their own rights. An adolescent may, for example, wish to learn more about evolution, sexuality, history, or religions of the world than his or her parents wish to permit. In cases such as these, parental authority, which ideally protects children's rights, comes into conflict with such rights.

Education By and For the Community

In discussing the freedoms of educational institutions, faculty, students, and parents (and potential conflicts among these), I have assumed a preexisting educational system. Educational systems are created by and for communities, however, and have ongoing obligations to those communities. A school or school system instituted by a religious or cultural group, for example, may justifiably be expected to serve the purposes of that group and to operate in accord with its beliefs and values.

The freedom of religious and other communities to educate in accord with their own beliefs, values, and purposes, however, does not eliminate the rationale for institutional and faculty autonomy, nor does it automatically override the right of students not to be indoctrinated and the authority of parents with regard to their own children.

Rather, the educational system of any community must, to be educationally and morally legitimate, properly balance a variety of rights, freedoms, interests, and responsibilities.

The situation is further complicated when the community in question is a multicultural democratic community responsible for a system of public education. Democratic public schools face all the community issues of any educational system plus two additional sets of complications. First, democratic public schools in a multicultural society have democratic obligations not to improperly promote or denigrate ultimate religious, political, or other doctrines. Second, the democratic community exists at multiple levels and is represented by multiple governmental entities.

The first set of complications concerns the democratic obligations of multicultural democratic societies and their schools. Democratic public education in a multicultural society may be regarded as a social contract in which democratic citizens agree to collectively educate the next generation without unjustifiably favoring or disfavoring any of the various philosophical, religious, moral, political, and other ultimate doctrines on which members of the current generation differ. This is not, it should be clear, a requirement of absolute neutrality. No educational system can be strictly neutral in all respects with regard to all doctrines. Deliberate deviations from neutrality, however, must be justified. Even unintended deviations from neutrality, if sufficiently systematic, may yield an undemocratic process of indoctrination. These considerations are particularly serious when the deviations from neutrality impinge on comprehensive or ultimate doctrines, such as religions.

When are deviations from neutrality justifiable? Some deviations from neutrality can be justified on educational or democratic grounds. Curricula may, for instance, favor well-justified scientific theories. They may also favor rational principles of human liberty and equality fundamental to any conception of democracy. Democratic public schools must not, however, deliberately or systematically promote or denigrate comprehensive religious, political, or other doctrines, regardless of whether those doctrines are widely esteemed or widely despised. There are thus important constraints on what democratic communities may expect or require their schools to do.

Like all educational institutions, democratic public schools violate the rights of students if they engage in indoctrination. The constraints on democratic public schools are stronger, however, than those on other schools. A school sponsored by a particular religious group, for example, may deliberately and systematically promote the beliefs and values of that religion and remain in accord with principles of academic freedom provided it does so in a nonindoctrinative manner in which students are free to disagree and to discuss alternative views and values. A democratic public school, on the contrary, must not deliberately and systematically promote a particular religion even if it does so with nonindoctrinative means.

Even to the extent that the democratic community has legitimate educational authority, there is a second set of complications. What constitutes the community? Is it the local community or some larger community? And who exercises democratic authority on behalf of that community?

In United States there is a long tradition of local control of public elementary and secondary education and state control of public higher education. Education at all levels, however, is influenced by state and national mandates, funding decisions, and political pressures. Educational authority is exercised in a variety of direct and indirect ways by local school boards; state school boards; college and university governing boards; state legislatures; the federal Department of Education; the U.S. Congress; and other elected and appointed officials at local, state, and national levels.

Community authority, expressed as governmental authority, takes us full circle to the need for institutional autonomy. Communities of all sorts have legitimate educational authority with regard to educational systems they choose to institute, but every community is nevertheless a permanent threat to intellectual freedom in its educational institutions. The urge to control the minds of the next generation is often too strong to resist.

Conclusion: Academic Freedom as Intellectual Freedom

Academic freedom, I have suggested, protects students, faculty, and educational institutions—and is closely related to the freedoms of parents and communities. These various freedoms, however, can (and regularly do) come into conflict. Whose freedom should prevail when there are disagreements among various combinations of students, parents, teachers, researchers, librarians, administrators, governing boards, community organizations, legislatures, and other elected and appointed officials? Unless we can specify how the various dimensions of academic freedom are to be coordinated, the concept of academic freedom may turn out to be incoherent. What if a teacher forbids or punishes the discussion of particular viewpoints on topics relevant to her class? Is she exercising her academic freedom? Can the faculty, acting collectively, require her to respect the academic freedom of her students? What if the faculty, acting collectively, forbid individual teachers to present particular topics or viewpoints? Can an administrator override this decision in order to protect the academic freedom of individual faculty? Can a school board require that something be included in the curriculum? Can a community? Who exactly has academic freedom, and when?

Academic freedom, I suggest, is not a right of any particular class of individuals to make all educational decisions. But if academic freedom protects everyone and everything, it may end up—due to its own incoherence—protecting no one and nothing. Instead, academic freedom is best construed as a complex of rights, freedoms, interests, and responsibilities centered on intellectual freedom. At its core, academic freedom is intellectual freedom in academic contexts. That is, *academic freedom is intellectual freedom in educational and research contexts.*

The legitimate exercise of authority in academic contexts, then, is always constrained by the responsibility to respect intellectual freedom. With regard to faculty, for example, the responsibility to avoid indoctrinating students is central to the ethics of teaching—and responsibility to the pursuit of truth is central to the ethics of research. Administrators and members of governing boards have corresponding ethical and professional responsibilities to maximize intellectual freedom for faculty and students. Students, in turn, should respect the intellectual freedom of their classmates, and parents should use their parental authority to enhance the educational opportunities of their children.

Academic freedom would have no real meaning if individual and collective autonomy and authority were overridden by any perceived deviation from perfect ethical and professional judgment. Nevertheless, there are limits. Academic freedom does not include a right of researchers to falsify their data, a right of teachers to indoctrinate their students, or a right of students to disrupt their classes. Nor does it include a right of administrators to substitute their personal opinions for the legitimate academic judgments of faculty, a right of democratic governing boards to impose their religious doctrines on public schools, or a right of communities to impose political doctrines on faculty and students.

Academic freedom is best understood not as a special privilege or ultimate authority of a particular class of individuals but as a set of principles of intellectual freedom that all individuals are obligated to respect in academic contexts. This obligation is generally a moral and educational one, based on the intellectual rights of students and the intellectual requirements of teaching, learning, inquiry, and development. We should respect academic freedom because students have a right not to be indoctrinated and because education and research require intellectual freedom.

A Legal Interlude

For public schools in the United States, there is an additional consideration: some aspects of academic freedom may be protected by the First Amendment. The constitutional history of academic freedom can be traced by highlighting four landmark First Amendment decisions of the U.S. Supreme Court.

The foundational case was *West Virginia v. Barnette* (1943). The question was stark and fundamental: Could public school students be required to salute the flag and pledge their allegiance? Although First Amendment law was still in its infancy, the court rejected the mandatory salute and pledge as unconstitutional. Freedom from indoctrination, argued Justice Robert Jackson in the plurality opinion, is guaranteed by the First Amendment, operating both as a protection of individual rights and as a structural requirement of democratic self-government. "We set up government by consent of the governed," wrote Justice Jackson, "and the Bill of Rights denies those in power any legal opportunity to coerce that consent" (641).

Over the next decade, anticommunist hysteria in the United States generated laws, loyalty oaths, and investigations all over the country—including systematic, ongoing programs to root out communists and communist ideas in public educational institutions. In *Keyishian v. Board of Regents* (1967), the U.S. Supreme Court ruled that New York State's anticommunist program was based on criteria so broad and vague as to unconstitutionally infringe on First Amendment freedoms of speech and association. Such infringements on intellectual freedom, the court concluded, are of special concern in educational contexts, where government is forbidden to "cast a pall of orthodoxy over the classroom" (603).

In *Tinker v. Des Moines* (1969), the court addressed the First Amendment rights of secondary school students to protest U.S. involvement in Vietnam by wearing black armbands to school. Even in the case of minors, ruled the court, students have First Amendment rights that they do not shed upon entering a school. They "may not be confined to the expression of those sentiments that are officially approved" (511). For nearly two decades, *Tinker* was applied by federal courts to protect freedom of expression in academic contexts.

In *Hazelwood v. Kuhlmeier* (1988), however, the court concluded that *Tinker* only applies to speech outside the curriculum. Within the curriculum, it ruled, schools have broad authority to censor and punish ideas they deem inconsistent with those the school is trying to teach. Although *Hazelwood* involved censorship of a high school newspaper, it has been applied by lower courts to student and faculty expression and discussion in multiple contexts at all levels of education, leading to a conception of education as a special context requiring special restrictions on intellectual freedom.

The Supreme Court's decision in *Morse v. Frederick* (2007), involving a "Bong Hits 4 Jesus" banner, was perhaps more of a bong hit than a legal landmark, but is nonetheless of considerable interest. In ruling once again for administrative authority over student expression, the court seemingly confirmed its retreat from the protection of First Amendment rights in public education. On closer analysis, however, "Bong Hits" can be read as a potentially important reaffirmation of *Tinker*, with a dubious but narrow exception concerning advocacy of illegal drug use.

Even to the extent that *Tinker* survives, however, so does *Hazelwood*. As we move to the defining core of the academic enterprise, the curriculum itself, the First Amendment becomes less and less applicable. Thus even in public schools we increasingly need a conception of academic freedom that does not rely on the First Amendment.

Such a conception is provided in Chapter 4. Yes, you can go right there. For a more detailed constitutional history of academic freedom you can read Chapters 2 and 3 on the way (I recommend them, of course). But the principles presented in Chapter 4 are not based on the First Amendment. They are consistent with it, and informed by the constitutional history, but they are rooted in the nature and needs of teaching, learning, inquiry, and development.

Chapter 2

The Constitutionalization of Academic Freedom

Issues of intellectual freedom in public education have been litigated in hundreds of cases in U.S. federal courts since the mid-twentieth century. Such cases range across interrelated matters of curriculum, methods of instruction, library acquisitions and removals, school newspapers and plays, and extracurricular activities. They raise issues of student expression, parental rights, faculty authority, and institutional autonomy. Arenas of controversy (both inside and outside the formal curriculum) include sexuality, evolution, religion, values, and cultural diversity. Cutting across elementary, secondary, and higher education, such cases highlight considerations of liberty, censorship, and indoctrination in democratic public schools.

U.S. federal courts routinely address intellectual freedom in public educational contexts with regard to the First Amendment rights of students, parents, teachers, researchers, and educational institutions themselves. The First Amendment to the U.S. Constitution, ratified in 1791, provides that

> Congress shall make no law respecting an establishment of religion, or prohibiting the free exercise thereof; or abridging the freedom of speech, or of the press; or the right of the people peaceably to assemble, and to petition the government for a redress of grievances.

Since the 1920s, the U.S. Supreme Court has construed the Fourteenth Amendment as extending the First Amendment to protect individuals against state, as well as federal, actions. In subsequent decades, the court formulated and elaborated constitutional principles critical to academic freedom and thus provided important legal protection against some egregious violations of intellectual freedom in U.S. public education. As we will see in Chapter 3, however, First

Amendment law since *Hazelwood v. Kuhlmeier* (1988) construes education as a special context in which the First Amendment has limited application. Thus, I will conclude, any defensible conception of academic freedom must protect far more than the constitutional minimum protected since *Hazelwood.*

West Virginia v. Barnette: Freedom from Indoctrination

When the fledgling American Association of University Professors (AAUP) issued its 1915 Declaration of Principles, academic freedom was already a concept and practice with a centuries-long history in Europe. The AAUP formulation, everyone understood, was intended as a guideline for the academic freedom of American professors, not as a legal doctrine.

The First Amendment, at that time, was a dead letter. States and their subdivisions, including public school boards, had always been free to restrict speech, press, and association as they chose. The federal government was theoretically subject to the First Amendment, but no federal restriction on speech, press, or association had ever been found unconstitutional; there was little reason to foresee that the First Amendment, or any other aspect of the Bill of Rights, would ever have more than rhetorical meaning.

What marks the beginning of academic freedom in U.S. constitutional law? Although it was not until 1943 (in *West Virginia v. Barnette*) that the Supreme Court established First Amendment rights in public education, two cases from the 1920s may be considered precursors to a constitutional conception of academic freedom.

World War I provoked an upsurge of anti-German sentiment throughout the United States. One of the forms this took was a 1919 Nebraska law specifying that

> no person, individually or as a teacher, shall, in any private, denominational, parochial, or public school, teach any subject to any person in any language [other] than the English language. . . . Languages, other than the English language, may be taught as languages only after a pupil shall have attained and successfully passed the eighth grade. . . . (quoted in *Meyer v. Nebraska* 1923, 397)

The Nebraska Supreme Court upheld the law but the U.S. Supreme Court reversed, concluding that it was inconsistent with the Fourteenth Amendment's general guarantee of liberty. Without invoking the First Amendment, the court ruled in *Meyer v. Nebraska* (1923) that the law was an unconstitutional attempt "to interfere with the calling of modern language teachers, with the opportunities of pupils to acquire knowledge, and with the power of parents to control the education of their own" (401).

About the same time, the Ku Klux Klan attempted to eliminate Catholic schools in Oregon by persuading the state to pass a law requiring that all children attend public schools. In *Pierce v. Society of Sisters* (1925), again without reference to the First Amendment, the U.S. Supreme Court found this law unconstitutional:

> The fundamental theory of liberty upon which all governments in this Union repose excludes any general power of the State to standardize its children by forcing them to accept instruction from public teachers only. The child is not the mere creature of the State; those who nurture him and direct his destiny have the right, coupled with the high duty, to recognize and prepare him for additional obligations. (535)

Although the decisions in *Meyer* and *Pierce* can be seen, in retrospect, as fully consistent with academic freedom, it is important to recall that, at the time these cases were decided, the First Amendment had not yet been applied to state governments. Despite the references quoted above to the rights of teachers, students, and parents, these decisions were based more on the economic interests of private schools than on considerations of intellectual freedom in education. Had the First Amendment not subsequently been applied to state governments, and ultimately to their educational functions, *Meyer* and *Pierce* would today stand for little more than the right of private schools to exist and to educate children in whatever language they please.

Beginning in 1925, however, the Supreme Court began to construe the First Amendment as applicable, through the due process clause of the Fourteenth Amendment, to state governments and their subdivisions. The First Amendment gradually took on real meaning in large part as a result of a series of cases involving the Jehovah's Witnesses. In the United States of the 1930s, Witnesses descended on communities like locusts, or so it seemed, with street-corner witnessing and door-to-door canvassing. They were, to say the least, very unpopular. And then, adding insult to injury, Witness schoolchildren refused to participate in compulsory flag salute exercises, which they and their families saw as contrary to the biblical command, "Thou shalt have no other gods before me.... Thou shalt not bow thyself down to them, nor serve them" (Exodus 20:3–5). When school authorities in Minersville, Pennsylvania, expelled twelve-year-old Lillian Gobitis and ten-year-old William Gobitis for refusing to salute the flag, their parents won judgments in lower federal courts that the requirement violated their religious beliefs. The Supreme Court reversed, however, ruling 8–1 that school children can be required to salute "the symbol of our national unity" (*Minersville v. Gobitis* 1940, 596). In lonely dissent, Chief Justice Harlan Fiske Stone argued for "the freedom of the individual from compulsion as to what he shall think and what he shall say, at least where the compulsion is to bear false witness to his religion" (604).

Gobitis was followed by hundreds of violent incidents across the country and by new flag salute requirements that aggravated the conflict. By 1943 more than two thousand Witness children had been expelled from schools and the Supreme Court was ready to reconsider.

The second flag salute case, *West Virginia v. Barnette* (1943), provided the constitutional foundation for academic freedom in the United States. Following the decision in *Gobitis*, the legislature of West Virginia amended its statutes to provide as follows:

> In all public, private, parochial and denominational schools located within this state there shall be given regular courses of instruction in history of the United States, in civics, and in the constitutions of the United States and of the State of West Virginia, for the purpose of teaching, fostering, and perpetuating the ideals, principles and spirit of Americanism. . . . (quoted in *West Virginia v. Barnette* 1943, footnote 1)

Following the legislature's patriotic lead, the West Virginia State Board of Education adopted a resolution in January 1942 requiring that all teachers and pupils in public schools salute the flag and pledge their allegiance as "a regular part of the program of activities." Lauding the flag as "the symbol of our national unity" and noting that "the public schools . . . are dealing with the formative period in the development in citizenship," the board specified that teachers and pupils must place their right hands on their breasts in "the commonly accepted salute to the flag of the United States" and repeat in unison "I pledge allegiance to the Flag of the United States of America and to the Republic for which it stands; one Nation, indivisible, with liberty and justice for all" (*West Virginia v. Barnette* 1943, footnote 2).

Failure to join in the flag salute and pledge of allegiance constituted "an act of insubordination" punishable by expulsion. Expelled
students could only be readmitted if they would agree to the salute
and pledge. If they would not, they were "unlawfully absent," which
could lead to delinquency proceedings against the child and prosecu-
tion of the parents.

A three-judge panel of the federal district court found the application of these requirements to Jehovah's Witnesses to be a violation
of their First Amendment right to religious freedom and freedom of
speech. The board of education appealed the decision directly to the
U.S. Supreme Court, which ruled 6–3 for the Witnesses. Justice Robert
Jackson's plurality opinion justified the decision on general grounds
of intellectual freedom and democratic self-government. Highlighting the educational context of the case, it set forth a First Amendment
right of nonindoctrination and thus a constitutional foundation for
academic freedom.

Central to the plurality was a conception of education as rational
teaching and learning. Such a conception, argued Justice Jackson, is
not inconsistent with patriotic outcomes. In the course of learning
about American history and government, for example, students might
be inspired to patriotic thoughts and feelings without any violation of
their "right of self-determination in matters that touch individual opinion and personal attitude" (631). But the present case was different:

> Here, however, we are dealing with a compulsion of students to
> declare a belief. They are not merely made acquainted with the flag
> salute so that they may be informed as to what it is or even what it
> means. The issue here is whether this slow and easily neglected
> route to aroused loyalties constitutionally may be short-cut by sub-
> stituting a compulsory salute and slogan. (631)

Addressing itself to this educational issue, the court noted an
important ambiguity:

> It is not clear whether the regulation contemplates that pupils
> forego any contrary convictions of their own and become unwill-
> ing converts to the prescribed ceremony or whether it will be
> acceptable if they simulate assent by words without belief and by a
> gesture barren of meaning. (633)

If the school will be satisfied with a meaningless gesture, this
requirement appears to serve no educational purpose. If, on the other

hand, the intent is to compel a change in beliefs, there is a question of whether indoctrination is a constitutionally legitimate form of education. Education may surely include "persuasion and example," but may it include "compulsion" (640)?

The plurality rejected indoctrination as inconsistent with (a) the constitutional basis for democratic government, (b) the special constitutional considerations relevant to a multicultural democracy, and (c) the First Amendment right of individuals to freedoms of belief and expression.

With regard to democratic government, the plurality saw indoctrination as a direct threat to values and assumptions at the core of the Constitution:

> There is no mysticism in the American concept of the State or of the nature or origin of its authority. We set up government by consent of the governed, and the Bill of Rights denies those in power any legal opportunity to coerce that consent. Authority here is to be controlled by public opinion, not public opinion by authority. (641)

Given that the persons whose opinions were threatened with coercion were children, this formulation suggests a construal of the Constitution as a contract across generations. Each generation may use the public educational system to convince the next of the value of democracy, but the convictions of the next generation must ultimately be self-determined, not the product of indoctrination.

The state argued that the exercise of saluting the flag and pledging allegiance in unison was designed to achieve national unity, a legitimate and important goal. Justice Jackson, however, rejected the assumption that the promotion of national unity requires coercion.

> National unity as an end which officials may foster by persuasion and example is not in question. The problem is whether under our Constitution compulsion as here employed is a permissible means for its achievement. (640)

The plurality acknowledged the cultural diversity that for many rendered the quest for national unity so urgent. It observed, however, that "struggles to coerce uniformity of sentiment" (640) have had devastating results throughout history.

> As governmental pressure toward unity becomes greater, so strife becomes more bitter as to whose unity it shall be. Probably no deeper division of our people could proceed from any provocation than from finding it necessary to choose what doctrine and whose program public educational officials shall compel youth to unite in embracing. (641)

Coercive efforts to achieve unity would undermine the actual and perceived legitimacy of schools. To the extent that public education imposes "ideological discipline," "each party or denomination must seek to control . . . the educational system" (637). Groups that perceive public education as a process of indoctrination in ideas and values inevitably contrary to their own will try to weaken the entire enterprise. The solution is for public schools to respect democratic principles of intellectual freedom: "Free public education, if faithful to the ideal of secular instruction and political neutrality, will not be partisan or enemy of any class, creed, party, or faction" (637).

But what about the community interest in social cohesion and patriotic commitment? Diversity and liberty, insisted the plurality, are not threats:

> We apply the limitations of the Constitution with no fear that freedom to be intellectually and spiritually diverse or even contrary will disintegrate the social organization. To believe that patriotism will not flourish if patriotic ceremonies are voluntary and spontaneous instead of a compulsory routine is to make an unflattering estimate of the appeal of our institutions to free minds. (641)

Highlighting "intellectual individualism" (641), Justice Jackson was clear that the concern for diversity included individual diversity and that the concern for the rights of the next generation included the rights of individual students. The First Amendment undergirded the opinion both as a structural requirement of any democratic system and as protection for individual rights to intellectual freedom. Indoctrination fails the test of constitutionality because it is inconsistent with democracy and with intellectual freedom. Democracy requires free minds, and is thus inconsistent with forms of schooling that "strangle the free mind at its source" (637).

Resolutely facing the radical implications of its analysis, the plurality was clear that respect for liberty must not be limited to trivial topics or minor disagreements:

Freedom to differ is not limited to things that do not matter much. That would be a mere shadow of freedom. The test of its substance is the right to differ as to things that touch the heart of the existing order.

If there is any fixed star in our constitutional constellation, it is that no official, high or petty, can prescribe what shall be orthodox in politics, nationalism, religion, or other matters of opinion or force citizens to confess by word or act their faith therein. If there are any circumstances which permit an exception, they do not now occur to us. (642)

Thus the right of students not to be indoctrinated is arguably, after *Barnette*, the constitutional core of academic freedom. For government to compel a compulsory salute and pledge "invades the sphere of intellect and spirit which it is the purpose of the First Amendment to our Constitution to reserve from all official control" (642).

The *Barnette* plurality rooted its ban on compulsory flag salutes and pledges in a more general right of individuals, including students, not to be indoctrinated by the government, and justified that right on the basis of democratic and First Amendment considerations. Inevitably there were ambiguities, even within the plurality opinion, with regard to the nature and scope of the right in question. The plurality opinion, moreover, did not represent a majority of the court. Although six of the nine justices joined the decision in favor of the Jehovah's Witnesses, they did not agree on a rationale. The opinion of Justice Jackson was joined by three other justices. The concurring opinion by Justices Hugo Black and William O. Douglas highlighted the religious freedom of the Witnesses rather than the more general right to intellectual individualism stressed by the plurality. Justices Black and Douglas pronounced themselves "substantially in agreement with the [plurality] opinion" (643) but did not join it. The fragmented opinion of the court thus added to the ambiguity regarding the nature and scope of the right not to be indoctrinated.

Keyishian v. Board of Regents: Intellectual Freedom in Education

In time, the Jehovah's Witnesses moderated their behavior and came to be seen as less of a threat. After World War II, there was a new hysteria—this time over an ideology deemed so pernicious that its eradication was a national priority. Fear of communism was not new, but beginning in the late 1940s anticommunism generated laws, loyalty oaths, and investigations that routinely violated fundamental freedoms of speech and association.

New York State addressed the concern about communist influence in education by passing the Feinberg Law, which added to the Education Law of the State of New York a new section entitled "Elimination of Subversive Persons from the Public School System." The new law provided for the board of regents, the superordinate governing board for the public schools of New York State, to compile a list of subversive organizations and to dismiss any teacher or school administrator who belonged to a listed organization or was found guilty of expressing subversive ideas.

In *Adler v. Board of Education* (1952), the U.S. Supreme Court upheld the constitutionality of the Feinberg Law. Justice William O. Douglas, joined by Justice Hugo Black, dissented, rejecting the Feinberg Law as inconsistent with the First Amendment. The dissent considered in some detail the effect of such a law on what it called, for the first time in the history of the U.S. Supreme Court, "academic freedom."

> The law inevitably turns the school system into a spying project. Regular loyalty reports on the teachers must be made out. The principals become detectives; the students, the parents, the community become informers. Ears are cocked for tell-tale signs of disloyalty. . . .
>
> What was the significance of the reference of the art teacher to socialism? Why was the history teacher so openly hostile to Franco's Spain? Who heard overtones of revolution in the English teacher's discussion of the *Grapes of Wrath*? What was behind the praise of Soviet progress in metallurgy in the chemistry class? Was it not "subversive" for the teacher to cast doubt on the wisdom of the venture in Korea?
>
> What happens under this law is typical of what happens in a police state. Teachers are under constant surveillance; their pasts are combed for signs of disloyalty; their utterances are watched for clues to dangerous thoughts. A pall is cast over the classrooms. There can be no real academic freedom in that environment. Where suspicion fills the air and holds scholars in line for fear of their jobs, there can be no exercise of the free intellect. Supineness and dogmatism take the place of inquiry. A "party line"—as dangerous as the "party line" of the Communists—lays hold. It is the "party line" of the orthodox view, of the conventional thought, of the accepted

approach. A problem can no longer be pursued with impunity to its edges. Fear stalks the classroom. The teacher is no longer a stimulant to adventurous thinking; she becomes instead a pipe line for safe and sound information. A deadening dogma takes the place of free inquiry. Instruction tends to become sterile; pursuit of knowledge is discouraged; discussion often leaves off where it should begin.

This, I think, is what happens when a censor looks over a teacher's shoulder. This system of spying and surveillance with its accompanying reports and trials cannot go hand in hand with academic freedom. It produces standardized thought, not the pursuit of truth. (509–511)

Thus the *Adler* dissent saw education as a social context requiring at least as much intellectual freedom as any other, and saw this need for academic freedom as mandating, in turn, that the First Amendment rights of teachers be fully protected: "The Constitution guarantees freedom of thought and expression to everyone in our society. All are entitled to it; and none needs it more than the teacher" (508).

Justices Douglas and Black expressed their support for academic freedom again five years later when, along with Justice William Brennan, they joined the plurality opinion by Chief Justice Earl Warren in *Sweezy v. New Hampshire* (1957). New Hampshire had in 1951 adopted a comprehensive scheme outlawing "subversive organizations" and forbidding the employment of "subversive persons" by any branch of the government, including public educational institutions. In a 1953 "Joint Resolution Relating to the Investigation of Subversive Activities," the legislature directed the state attorney general "to make full and complete investigation with respect to violations of the subversive activities act of 1951 and to determine whether subversive persons as defined in said act are presently located within this state" (quoted in *Sweezy v. New Hampshire* 1957, 236–237). The attorney general used this authority to institute hearings around the state and to subpoena a number of individuals, including many faculty at Dartmouth and the University of New Hampshire.

Economist Paul Sweezy, who had left a position at Harvard and was now living in New Hampshire, was interrogated by the attorney general in January 1954 and again that June. In a written statement he indicated that he had "studied the subversive activities act of 1951 with care" and had "absolutely no knowledge of any violations of any of its provisions" and "no knowledge of subversive persons presently located within the state." He stated that he would answer some questions about himself but would "respectfully decline to answer questions concerning ideas, beliefs, and associations which could not possibly be pertinent to the matter here under inquiry and/or which seem to me to invade the freedoms guaranteed by the First Amendment" (quoted in *Sweezy v. New Hampshire* 1957, footnote 6).

Sweezy answered most of the many questions put to him, acknowledging that he considered himself a "classical Marxist" and a "socialist" but denying that he advocated the violent overthrow of constitutional government or had ever been a member of the Communist Party. Consistent with his written statement, however, he refused to answer questions about his involvement in the Progressive Party and, most relevant for our purposes, questions about a lecture he had given—his third in three years—to a class at the University of New Hampshire. Hauled into court, he refused again to answer these questions and was found in contempt, a determination subsequently affirmed by the New Hampshire Supreme Court.

In *Sweezy v. New Hampshire* (1957), the U.S. Supreme Court reversed. The six justices who constituted the majority could not agree on a rationale, however. There were three distinct opinions from the eight justices who participated in the case—a plurality opinion representing four of the justices, a concurring opinion representing two more, and a dissent representing the remaining two justices.

The plurality, consistent with the *Adler* dissent, saw both a general First Amendment problem and a special need to attend to academic freedom:

> It is particularly important that the exercise of the power of compulsory process be carefully circumscribed when the investigative process tends to impinge upon such highly sensitive areas as freedom of speech or press, freedom of political association, and freedom of communication of ideas, particularly in the academic community. (245)

The case for academic freedom is especially strong, the justices thought, at the level of higher education:

> The essentiality of freedom in the community of American universities is almost self-evident. No one should underestimate the vital role in a democracy that is played by those who guide and train our youth. To impose any strait jacket upon the intellectual leaders

in our colleges and universities would imperil the future of our nation. . . . Scholarship cannot flourish in an atmosphere of suspicion and distrust. Teachers and students must always remain free to inquire, to study and to evaluate, to gain new maturity and understanding; otherwise our civilization will stagnate and die. (250)

The plurality found "that there unquestionably was an invasion of petitioner's liberties in the areas of academic freedom and political expression" (250). Without conceiving "any circumstance wherein a state interest would justify infringement of rights in these fields," the justices saw no need "to reach such fundamental questions of state power" (251). Instead, turning to issues of due process, the plurality concluded that the discretion of the attorney general was so great, and the connection of the present lines of interrogation to legislative authorization so tenuous, that, given the First Amendment rights at stake, the use of the contempt power to compel Sweezy's testimony was unconstitutional.

Justice Felix Frankfurter, joined by Justice John Marshall Harlan II, concurred in the result but wrote a separate opinion. With regard to the three lectures, the concurring opinion was more concerned with the institutional autonomy of the University of New Hampshire than with the rights of Paul Sweezy. "When weighed against the grave harm resulting from governmental intrusion into the intellectual life of a university," argued Justice Frankfurter, the justifications accepted by the New Hampshire Supreme Court for compelling Sweezy to discuss the contents of his lecture were "grossly inadequate" (261). The unquestionable "dependence of a free society on free universities" entails "the exclusion of governmental intervention in the intellectual life of a university" (262). This includes not only direct interventions but investigations of the present sort that "check the ardor and fearlessness of scholars, qualities at once so fragile and so indispensable for fruitful academic labor" (262).

Quoting extensively from a statement of South African scholars, Justice Frankfurter noted that "in a university knowledge is its own end, not merely a means to an end" (262) and that "the concern of its scholars is not merely to add and revise facts in relation to an accepted framework, but to be ever examining and modifying the framework itself" (263). For a university to be thus "characterized by the spirit of free inquiry" (262), the government must respect "'the four essential freedoms' of a university—to determine for itself on academic grounds who may teach, what may be taught, how it shall be taught, and who may be admitted to study" (263).

It is fair to say, then, that a majority of the court found the questioning of Sweezy about his lectures inconsistent with academic freedom. The plurality and concurring opinions highlighted different aspects of academic freedom, however—the former focusing on the individual rights of the teacher and the latter on the institutional autonomy of the university. The two opinions were sufficiently different, in fact, that it remained unclear whether there was some coherent conception of academic freedom that the court had found (or would find) to be protected by the First Amendment.

A decade later, in *Keyishian v. Board of Regents* (1967), a narrow but unambiguous majority of the court pronounced academic freedom to be "a special concern of the First Amendment" (603). At issue once again, fifteen years after *Adler*, was New York's Feinberg Law and associated statutes, amendments, and regulations designed to root out communism in the state government, including the public educational system. Several faculty at the State University of New York in Buffalo faced dismissal because they refused to certify that they were not members of the Communist Party and that, if they ever had been, they had communicated this fact, as legally required, to the president of the State University of New York. A three-judge federal court rejected their claim that the state program of identifying subversive teachers and removing them from the public schools was unconstitutional.

The Supreme Court reversed, ruling 5–4 that New York's program was based on criteria so broad and so vague as to unconstitutionally infringe on First Amendment freedoms of speech and association. The majority opinion by Justice William Brennan, acknowledging that the court had earlier rejected a challenge to the Feinberg Law (*Adler v. Board of Education* [1952], discussed above), ruled that *Adler* did not control the present case for two reasons. First, *Keyishian* raised issues of vagueness that had not been comprehensively addressed in *Adler*. Second, the decision in *Adler* was rooted in doctrines that had been rejected in subsequent years. In particular, Supreme Court decisions since *Adler* had extended First Amendment protection to encompass membership in organizations with unlawful aims, provided the member did not specifically intend to further those aims, and had established that government employment could not be conditioned on waiving one's First Amendment rights. Thus mere membership in the

Communist Party, even if the Communist Party included among its aims the violent overthrow of the United States government, could not be criminalized and could not be a disqualification for government employment.

The majority noted several examples of vague language in provisions associated with the Feinberg Law. It was concerned, for instance, with a requirement that a teacher or administrator be dismissed "for the utterance of any treasonable or seditious word or words or the doing of any treasonable or seditious act or acts" (quoted in *Keyishian v. Board of Regents* 1967, 612). Definitions provided in the law, the court concluded, were insufficient to establish the meaning of this phrase with adequate clarity:

> The teacher cannot know the extent, if any, to which a "seditious" utterance must transcend mere statement about abstract doctrine, the extent to which it must be intended to and tend to indoctrinate or incite to action in furtherance of the defined doctrine. The crucial consideration is that no teacher can know just where the line is drawn between "seditious" and nonseditious utterances and acts. (599)

In fact, observed the court, given the intricate network of interconnected provisions associated with the Feinberg Law, a teacher might reasonably fear termination for carrying a copy of the Communist Manifesto in public or for teaching students about the U.S. Declaration of Independence—which does, after all, propose grounds for the forceful overthrow of governments.

The court noted, moreover, that the Feinberg Law required "annual review of every teacher to determine whether any utterance or act of his, inside the classroom or out, came within the sanctions of the laws" (602) as part of its "intricate administrative machinery for . . . enforcement" (601). The combination of vague criteria and intimidating process would, the court concluded, have a chilling effect on education:

> It would be a bold teacher who would not stay as far as possible from utterances or acts which might jeopardize his living by enmeshing him in this intricate machinery. The uncertainty as to the utterances and acts proscribed increases that caution. . . . The result must be to stifle "that free play of the spirit which all teachers ought especially to cultivate and practice. . . ." (601)

In reaching and justifying its decision, the court could have focused on rights general to all government employees but chose not to do so. Alternatively, it could have distinguished *Keyishian* from *Adler* by emphasizing that the present case arose in the context of higher education and arguing, on the basis of *Sweezy*, that universities or their faculty require special protection with regard to intellectual freedom. It did not choose this route either. Justice Brennan's majority opinion highlighted the fact that the government employees in the present case were teachers but conspicuously ignored the fact that they taught at a university. Freedoms of expression and association were deemed to have special relevance at all levels of education. That teachers are responsible for "captive audiences of young minds" (607) is not reason to restrict their intellectual liberties. On the contrary, the social role and societal value of education mandate especially stringent protection of intellectual freedom in all educational contexts:

> Our nation is deeply committed to safeguarding academic freedom, which is of transcendent value to all of us and not merely to the teachers concerned. That freedom is therefore a special concern of the First Amendment, which does not tolerate laws that cast a pall of orthodoxy over the classroom. (603)

Chapter 3

From Armbands to Bong Hits in the U.S. Supreme Court

hapter 2 provided a constitutional history of academic freedom through the Supreme Court's 1967 decision in *Keyishian v. Board of Regents*. We now continue that history. As we will see, the next major decision came just two years later but reflected a shift in focus from McCarthyism to Vietnam, and from teachers to students.

Tinker v. Des Moines: Freedom of Expression

In December 1965, fifteen-year-old John Tinker, his thirteen-year-old sister Mary Beth Tinker, and sixteen-year-old Christopher Eckhardt were suspended from their public schools in Des Moines, Iowa, for wearing black armbands to express their opposition to the U.S. military intervention in Vietnam. They sued in federal court, arguing that such censorship violated their First Amendment rights. A district court dismissed the complaint and this decision was upheld on appeal. In *Tinker v. Des Moines* (1969), on a 7–2 vote, the Supreme Court reversed. Citing both *Barnette* and *Keyishian*, it ruled that "students are entitled to freedom of expression of their views" (511).

The majority opinion by Justice Abe Fortas acknowledged "the comprehensive authority of the States and of school officials, consistent with fundamental constitutional safeguards, to prescribe and control conduct in the schools" (507). With regard to expressive conduct, it granted that the First Amendment must be "applied in light of the special characteristics of the school environment" (506). Nevertheless, insisted the court, "it can hardly be argued that either students or teachers shed their constitutional rights to freedom of speech or expression at the schoolhouse gate" (506).

The court noted that "this case does not concern speech or action that intrudes upon the work of the schools or the rights of other students" (508). Although the district court had "concluded that the action of the school authorities was reasonable because it was based upon their fear of a disturbance from the wearing of the armbands" (508), the Supreme Court concluded that the claimed fear of disturbance was likely a cover for "an urgent wish to avoid ... controversy" (510). Even if the fear of disturbance was genuine, moreover, "the record fails to yield evidence that the school authorities had reason to anticipate that the wearing of the armbands would substantially interfere with the work of the school or impinge upon the rights of other students" (509). School officials have authority to prevent disruptions of education, but when First Amendment rights are at stake assertions of potential disruption must be genuine and well supported:

> In our system, undifferentiated fear or apprehension of disturbance is not enough to overcome the right to freedom of expression. Any departure from absolute regimentation may cause trouble. Any variation from the majority's opinion may inspire fear. Any word spoken, in class, in the lunchroom, or on the campus, that deviates from the views of another person may start an argument or cause a disturbance. But our Constitution says we must take this risk. . . .
>
> In order for the State in the person of school officials to justify prohibition of a particular expression of opinion, it must be able to show that its action was caused by something more than a mere desire to avoid the discomfort and unpleasantness that always accompany an unpopular viewpoint. Certainly where there is no finding and no showing that engaging in the forbidden conduct would "materially and substantially interfere with the requirements of appropriate discipline in the operation of the school," the prohibition cannot be sustained. (508–509)

Moreover, in a passage reminiscent of *Barnette*, the court went on to present student freedom of expression as not just a right of individual students but an important safeguard against indoctrination:

> In our system, state-operated schools may not be enclaves of totalitarianism. School officials do not possess absolute authority over their students. Students ... may not be regarded as closed-circuit recipients of only that which the State chooses to communicate. They may not be confined to the expression of those sentiments that are officially approved. (511)

Student expression, concluded the court, is "an important part of the educational process" (512) and must not be "so circumscribed that it exists in principle but not in fact" (513). For a decade or more after 1969, courts applying *Tinker* provided genuine and substantial First Amendment protection to students and faculty at all levels of public education.

Hazelwood v. Kuhlmeier: School Authority over Curriculum

Although *Barnette*, *Sweezy*, *Keyishian*, and *Tinker* clearly established a constitutional basis for academic freedom in the United States, all four decisions included vigorous dissents. The primary concern was that the constitutionalization of academic freedom is a threat to the legitimate exercise of educational authority by governments and school officials. In general, rather than invoke First Amendment rights, courts should defer to the judgments of educational officials. In the 1980s, at least with regard to matters of curriculum, the dissenting view prevailed.

The divisions within the Supreme Court were particularly evident in *Board of Education v. Pico* (1982), a case in which members of the school board in Island Trees, New York, having returned from a conference with a list of "objectionable" books, arranged for a janitor to let them into a school library at night so they could check the contents of the library against their list. The board ultimately directed the removal of eleven books, appointed a committee to review the books, and then—ignoring the committee's advice—made most of the removals permanent.

Several students sued in federal court, arguing that the book removals violated their First Amendment rights. The district court saw no legitimate First Amendment claim and issued a summary judgment supporting the school board's authority with regard to schoolbooks. A court of appeals, concluding that there was indeed a genuine First Amendment issue, remanded the case for a full trial to determine whether the First Amendment had in fact been violated.

The Supreme Court, voting 5–4 to uphold the decision to remand the case to district court for a full trial, issued seven distinct opinions—none of which commanded a majority of the court. Four justices supported the view that there was indeed a potential First Amendment issue and thus a need for a full trial, but could not agree on what criteria would have to be met for the book removals to violate the First Amendment. Four justices, for a variety of interlocking reasons, agreed with the district court that there was no First Amendment issue and thus no need for a trial. The ninth justice upheld on procedural grounds the decision of the appeals court to remand for trial and explicitly declined to address the First Amendment question. Further litigation was avoided when the school board subsequently voted to return the books to the library, but the Supreme Court's profound ambivalence was clear.

The court was less ambivalent in *Bethel v. Fraser* (1986) when it voted 7–2 to reject a First Amendment challenge in a case where a high school had punished a student for the humorous sexual content of a brief speech supporting a candidate in a school election (see Case 9–4). Even in the absence of disruption, ruled the court, school officials could enforce standards of "civility" (681). It was unclear, however, whether this retreat from *Tinker* was a limited exception applicable primarily to sexual speech or the precursor of a more general retreat from application of the First Amendment in educational contexts.

In *Hazelwood v. Kuhlmeier* (1988), the court clarified that the retreat was general. Without overturning *Tinker*, it drastically narrowed its scope to "personal expression that happens to occur on the school premises" (271). In a major victory for governmental and administrative discretion, the court construed the curriculum, and all speech associated with it, as a domain largely outside the scope of the First Amendment. Acknowledging that "neither students nor teachers shed their constitutional rights to freedom of speech or expression at the schoolhouse gate" (*Tinker v. Des Moines* 1969, 506), the court determined, in effect, that they shed those rights at the classroom door.

In the 1982–1983 academic year, Cathy Kuhlmeier, Leslie Smart, and Leanne Tippett were staff members of *Spectrum*, the school newspaper of Hazelwood East High School in St. Louis County, Missouri. *Spectrum* "was written and edited by the Journalism II class at Hazelwood East" (*Hazelwood v. Kuhlmeier* 1988, 262). In May 1983 the principal removed a page from the final issue prior to publication because two of the six articles on that page were deemed objectionable. "One of the stories described three Hazelwood East students' experiences with pregnancy; the other discussed the impact of divorce on students at the school" (263). The principal was concerned about the privacy of individuals who were named or might be identifiable and "believed that the article's references to sexual activity and birth control were inappropriate for some of the younger students at the school" (263).

The students sued in federal court. The district court ruled that the principal had acted within his authority but the Court of Appeals for the Eighth Circuit reversed, ruling on the basis of *Tinker* that the First Amendment rights of the students had been violated. The Supreme Court reversed once again, ruling 5–3 for the school.

The majority opinion by Justice Byron White construed *Tinker* narrowly to mean only that students generally "cannot be punished merely for expressing their personal views on the school premises" (266). Correspondingly, it interpreted *Bethel v. Fraser* broadly to stand for the general proposition that "'the determination of what manner of speech in the classroom or in school assembly is inappropriate properly rests with the school board'... rather than with the federal courts" (267, quoting from *Bethel v. Fraser* 1986, 683). Unless a public forum has been specifically created, "school officials may impose reasonable restrictions on the speech of students, teachers, and other members of the school community" (*Hazelwood* 1988, 267). Because *Spectrum* was part of the journalism curriculum, concluded the court, *Tinker* did not apply. "School officials were entitled to regulate the contents of *Spectrum* in any reasonable manner" (270).

In other words, curriculum decisions (including those involving censorship of student and faculty expression) need only satisfy the very minimal constitutional requirement that they be "reasonable"— the judicial standard for judging governmental actions that do not implicate fundamental rights. The First Amendment, concluded the *Hazelwood* majority, has little relevance to decisions about what will be taught and about what students and teachers may say and write in the course of

> expressive activities that students, parents, and members of the public might reasonably perceive to bear the imprimatur of the school. These activities may fairly be characterized as part of the school curriculum, whether or not they occur in a traditional classroom setting, so long as they are supervised by faculty members and designed to impart particular knowledge or skills to student participants and audiences.
>
> Educators are entitled to exercise greater control over this second form of student expression to assure that participants learn whatever lessons the activity is designed to teach, that readers or listeners are not exposed to material that may be inappropriate for their level of maturity, and that the views of the individual speaker are not erroneously attributed to the school. Hence, a school may in

its capacity as publisher of a school newspaper or producer of a school play "disassociate itself" [quoting from *Bethel v. Fraser* 1986, 685] not only from speech that would "substantially interfere with [its] work . . . or impinge upon the rights of other students" [quoting from *Tinker v. Des Moines* 1969, 509], but also from speech that is, for example, ungrammatical, poorly written, inadequately researched, biased or prejudiced, vulgar or profane, or unsuitable for immature audiences. . . . A school must also retain the authority to refuse to sponsor student speech that might reasonably be perceived to advocate drug or alcohol use, irresponsible sex, or conduct otherwise inconsistent with "the shared values of a civilized social order" [quoting from *Bethel v. Fraser* 1986, 683], or to associate the school with any position other than neutrality on matters of political controversy. (*Hazelwood v. Kuhlmeier* 1988, 271–272)

Concluded the court:

Educators to do not offend the First Amendment by exercising editorial control over the style and content of student speech in school-sponsored expressive activities so long as their actions are reasonably related to legitimate pedagogical concerns. (273)

The side of the students was taken by the court's three eldest justices. The dissenting opinion by Justice William Brennan, joined by Justices Thurgood Marshall and Harry Blackmun, provided a forceful argument that the principal had engaged in an act of censorship that violated the First Amendment rights of the student journalists.

"Free student expression," acknowledged the dissent, "undoubtedly sometimes interferes with the effectiveness of the school's pedagogical functions" (279). Justice Brennan suggested a distinction, however, between expression "directly preventing the school from pursuing its pedagogical mission" and speech that "frustrates the school's legitimate pedagogical purposes merely by expressing a message that conflicts with the school's" (279). A student who insists on giving a political speech during a calculus class directly "interferes with the legitimate teaching of calculus" whereas a student who praises socialism in response to a question in a political science class is not "directly interfering with the school's expression of its message" even if the student's expression of opinion "subverts the school's inculcation of the message that capitalism is better" (279).

Without denying school authority over the curriculum, the dissent rejected the view that schools may limit students to speech consistent with the curriculum:

> If mere incompatibility with the school's pedagogical message were a constitutionally sufficient justification for the suppression of student speech, school officials could censor [a great deal of student expression], converting our public schools into "enclaves of totalitarianism" [quoting *Tinker* 1969, 511] that "strangle the free mind at its source" [quoting *West Virginia v. Barnette* 1943, 637]. The First Amendment permits no such blanket censorship authority. . . . Public educators must accommodate some student expression even if it offends them or offers views or values that contradict those the school wishes to inculcate. (280)

The majority's distinction between personal and school-sponsored expression, Justice Brennan pointed out, was unprecedented in constitutional law. The court's decision, he argued, "erects a taxonomy of school censorship" (281). *Tinker*, and thus First Amendment law, govern "censorship 'to silence a student's personal expression that happens to occur on the school premises,'" (281, quoting from the majority opinion). School authority prevails for expression associated with the curriculum.

Justice Brennan rejected the majority's "taxonomy of school censorship" as a needless effort to solve a problem that had already been solved. The proper balance of respect for student rights and for the needs of education had been struck in *Tinker*. The majority's reasons for extending the scope of official control over student expression were woefully inadequate:

> The court offers no more than an obscure tangle of three excuses to afford educators "greater control" over school-sponsored speech than the *Tinker* test would permit: the public educator's prerogative to control curriculum; the pedagogical interest in shielding the high school audience from objectionable viewpoints and sensitive topics; and the school's need to dissociate itself from student expression. . . . None of the excuses, once disentangled, supports the distinction that the court draws. *Tinker* fully addresses the first concern; the second is illegitimate; and the third is readily achievable through less oppressive means. (282–283)

With regard to control of curriculum, the dissent saw the material disruption standard set in *Tinker* as sufficient:

> Manifestly, student speech is more likely to disrupt a curricular function when it arises in the context of a curricular activity. . . . Thus, under *Tinker*, the school may constitutionally punish the budding political orator if he disrupts calculus class but not if he holds his tongue for the cafeteria. . . . That is not because some more stringent standard applies in the curricular context. (After all, this court applied the same standard whether the students in *Tinker* wore their armbands to the "classroom" or the "cafeteria" [citing *Tinker* 1969, 512].) It is because student speech in the noncurricular context is less likely to disrupt materially any legitimate pedagogical purpose. (283)

The dissent did not doubt that "the educator may, under *Tinker*, constitutionally 'censor' poor grammar, writing, or research because to reward such expression would 'materially disrup[t]' the newspaper's curricular purpose" (284). On the basis of the record, however, the dissent dismissed as "utterly incredible" (285) the supposition of the majority that the principal intended to provide a pedagogical lesson. Far from receiving journalistic feedback and guidance, it noted, the students first learned of the deletions when the paper was released. Even after they protested, the principal "explained the deletions only in the broadest of generalities" (285). In one meeting, for example, "he deemed [the articles] simply 'inappropriate, personal, sensitive and unsuitable for the newspaper'" (285, quoting from the district court decision).

Having dismissed the principal's action as censorship, not education, the dissent saw no greater merit in the majority's second line of argument:

> The court's second excuse for deviating from precedent is the school's interest in shielding an impressionable high school audience from material whose substance is "unsuitable for immature audiences." . . . Specifically, the majority decrees that we must afford educators authority to shield high school students from exposure to "potentially sensitive topics" . . . or unacceptable social viewpoints. . . . [quoting from the majority opinion].
>
> *Tinker* teaches us that the state educator's undeniable, and undeniably vital, mandate to inculcate moral and political values is not

a general warrant to act as "thought police" stifling discussion of all but state-approved topics and advocacy of all but the official position. . . . Otherwise educators could transform students into "closed-circuit recipients of only that which the State chooses to communicate" [citing *Tinker* 1969, 511], and cast a perverse and impermissible "pall of orthodoxy over the classroom" [citing *Keyishian* 1967, 603]. (*Hazelwood* 1988, 286)

"Thought control in the high school," continued the dissent, may consist of (a) "school suppression of disfavored viewpoints" or (b) "official assessment of topic sensitivity" (286). The former is "unabashed and unconstitutional viewpoint discrimination" (286–287). As for the latter, "'potential topic sensitivity' is a vaporous nonstandard . . . that invites manipulation . . . and chills student speech" (287). Content discrimination is inevitable in education—a given course, activity, or publication may be limited to a particular topic, and the quality of student work may be evaluated, with consequences for the student—but this does not justify viewpoint discrimination, or vague standards that are likely to serve as a cover for viewpoint discrimination.

With respect to the third excuse for increasing official control over student expression beyond what *Tinker* would permit, the dissent acknowledged the legitimate concern "'that the views of the individual speaker [might be] erroneously attributed to the school'" (288, quoting from the majority opinion). Such misattributions may be prevented, however, through means less restrictive than suppressing student speech. With respect to a school newspaper, for example, the paper might simply be required to publish a routine disclaimer that the school does not control, and is thus not responsible for, the content of the paper. More generally, a school may dissociate itself from student expression by issuing responses clarifying its positions and explaining why students are wrong. "Yet, without so much as acknowledging the less oppressive alternatives," observed the dissent, "the court approves of brutal censorship" (289).

The dissent concluded that the present case should have been judged against the standards set forth in *Tinker*. Lacking any reason to believe that publication of the articles in question would have disrupted education or violated anyone's legal rights, the principal had no constitutional authority to delete them. The fact that he "did not so much as inquire into obvious alternatives [showed an] unthinking contempt for individual rights [that] is intolerable from any state official" (290). And the Supreme Court itself, abandoning its own precedents, had joined in the lesson:

> The court opens its analysis in this case by purporting to reaffirm *Tinker*'s time-tested proposition that public school students "do not 'shed their constitutional rights to freedom of speech or expression at the schoolhouse gate'" [quoting the majority quoting *Tinker*]. That is an ironic introduction to an opinion that denudes high school students of much of the First Amendment protection that *Tinker* itself prescribed. Instead of "teach[ing] children to respect the diversity of ideas that is fundamental to the American system" [quoting *Board of Education v. Pico* 1982, 880, Blackmun, J., concurring], and "that our Constitution is a living reality, not parchment preserved under glass" [citation omitted], the court today "teach[es] youth to discount important principles of our government as mere platitudes" [quoting *West Virginia v. Barnette* 1943, 637]. (*Hazelwood* 1988, 290–291, Brennan, J., dissenting)

In the years since 1988, applications of *Hazelwood* in the lower courts have severely constricted the scope of First Amendment rights in U.S. public education. The majority opinion took the school newspaper to be an extension of the curriculum and proceeded to expand the authority of school officials to regulate and restrict student and faculty expression in all curricular contexts. It explicitly left open the question of *Hazelwood*'s relevance to colleges and universities (*Hazelwood*, footnote 7).

Justice Brennan recognized that *Hazelwood* "denudes high school students of much of the First Amendment protection that *Tinker* . . . prescribed" (290). Within three years the U.S. Court of Appeals for the Eleventh Circuit had, on the basis of *Hazelwood*, concluded that a university "has dominion over what is taught by its professors and may so manage them" (*Bishop v. Aronov* 1991, 1078). Subsequent decisions have confirmed the broad authority of school officials with regard to curriculum-related expressive activities of students and faculty at all levels of education.

Students and faculty still have some First Amendment rights. Extracurricular student expression, in particular, has continued to enjoy substantial First Amendment protection. Speech codes are common but rarely survive legal challenges. Voluntary student groups must be granted access to facilities and resources without discrimination on the basis of viewpoint. The Supreme Court has, moreover, continued to interpret the First Amendment ban on the establishment of religion to require special constraints on religious indoctrination (see Chapter 11). Nevertheless, *Hazelwood* can be considered the end of the line for constitutional academic freedom—that is, for the conception elaborated in *Barnette, Sweezy, Keyishian*, and *Tinker* that education is a special context requiring special protection of intellectual freedom and thus strict application of the First Amendment. *Hazelwood* initiates a new scheme that is essentially the mirror image of academic freedom. Education is now construed as a special realm largely outside the scope of First Amendment protection.

Morse v. Frederick: Bong Hits 4 Jesus

In January 2002 the Olympic torch relay, en route to the winter games in Salt Lake City, Utah, came through Juneau, Alaska, while schools were in session, on a street that ran right by Juneau-Douglas High School. Students, supervised by school staff, were permitted to observe the procession from both sides of the street. One student, Joseph Frederick, aware that national media were filming the event, sought to attract their attention by unfurling a fourteen-foot banner that read "Bong Hits 4 Jesus." Principal Deborah Morse ordered him to take the banner down and, when he failed to do so, confiscated it and suspended him for ten days. Frederick sued and eventually won a judgment from the Ninth Circuit Court of Appeals that, under *Tinker*, his First Amendment rights had been violated. In June 2007 the Supreme Court reversed.

There were no less than five opinions in "Bong Hits." Chief Justice John Roberts wrote the majority opinion, signed by Justices Clarence Thomas, Antonin Scalia, Samuel Alito, and Anthony Kennedy. Justice Thomas also wrote a concurring opinion of his own, as did Justice Alito (who was joined by Justice Kennedy). Justice Stephen Breyer wrote an opinion concurring in part and not reaching the First Amendment issue. Justice John Paul Stevens, who was somewhat uncharacteristically part of the majority in *Hazelwood*, wrote a dissent joined by Justices David Souter and Ruth Bader Ginsburg.

The majority opinion held that public schools may censor and punish students who, contrary to school policy, advocate the use of illegal drugs. The decision was limited to the particular topic (illegal drugs) and viewpoint (use them). Importantly, the court explicitly rejected arguments, based on language in *Bethel v. Fraser* (1986), that schools have general authority to ban "offensive" speech.

In his concurring opinion, Justice Thomas waxed nostalgic for the good old days of the nineteenth century when "teachers taught, and students listened. Teachers commanded, and students obeyed." He argued that students have no First Amendment rights whatsoever, that *Tinker* was wrongly decided, and that the court should simply repudiate it and be done with all this nonsense about student rights. No other justice joined this concurrence; the other eight all unambiguously accepted *Tinker* as established precedent.

The concurring opinion by Justice Alito, joined by Justice Kennedy, is what in another context might be called a "signing statement." Justices Alito and Kennedy insisted that they joined the majority opinion with the understanding that it was strictly limited to advocacy of illegal drug use and provided no support whatsoever for restricting speech on any political or social issue, including issues such as the "war on drugs." They explicitly noted that the court had not endorsed the arguments of the school district and of the Bush administration that school authorities may censor any speech that interferes with the school's "educational mission." Thus Justices Alito and Kennedy, both of whose votes were necessary for the majority, insisted on a narrow reading of the opinion.

Justice Breyer essentially abstained on the ground that the court should avoid important constitutional questions whenever a case can be resolved some other way. He joined the court's unanimous judgment that the principal had not so clearly violated a clearly established right to be personally liable, but argued that the case should be sent back to a lower court for further proceedings—which could resolve all remaining issues without reaching the First Amendment question.

Justice Stevens, joined by Justices Souter and Ginsburg, dissented, maintaining that Frederick was protected by the First Amendment. His banner, the dissent insisted, did not advocate anything at all. Even if it did, there was no exception for speech about drugs in First Amendment law, and no reason to carve one out.

Overall, the "Bong Hits" majority wasn't high on the First Amendment but their decision wasn't the mind-blowing bummer feared by fans of *Tinker*. As for Joseph Frederick, all he ever wanted was national publicity. Obviously, he got it.

Conclusion

Tinker lives on, as we have just seen, but so does *Hazelwood*. The *Tinker* decision was rooted in general principles of First Amendment law and required no special appeal to academic freedom. Nevertheless, the court took special notice of the academic context of the case and developed a supplementary line of argument to justify its conclusion specifically on grounds of academic freedom. Noting that cases such as *Keyishian* had emphasized the special importance of intellectual freedom in education, the court argued for a broad construal of educational processes that includes communication among students throughout the school day:

> The principle of these cases is not confined to the supervised and ordained discussion which takes place in the classroom. The principal use to which the schools are dedicated is to accommodate students during prescribed hours for the purpose of certain types of activities. Among those activities is personal intercommunication among the students [footnote omitted]. This is not only an inevitable part of the process of attending school; it is also an important part of the educational process. A student's rights, therefore, do not embrace merely the classroom hours. (*Tinker v. Des Moines* 1969, 512)

Operating from a premise of academic freedom, the *Tinker* court extended what it took to be the well-established protection of First Amendment rights within curricular contexts to reinforce the general First Amendment protection of extracurricular expression. The *Hazelwood* court, in contrast, began with the unexamined and unjustified premise that the curriculum is essentially a First Amendment–free zone. Construing the school newspaper as part of the journalism curriculum, then, did not bring into play some special regard for intellectual freedom. On the contrary, the curricular context eliminated even the general protections of the First Amendment and thus settled the issue in favor of school authority.

Both *Tinker* and *Hazelwood*, in other words, construe education as a special context with regard to intellectual freedom, but in opposite senses. *Tinker*, following the academic freedom tradition of *Barnette*, *Sweezy*, and *Keyishian*, construes education as a special domain requiring especially stringent protection of First Amendment rights. *Hazelwood*, in contrast, construes education as a special domain largely beyond the scope of the First Amendment.

Why should the First Amendment not apply to education? Echoing themes from the lengthy and vigorous dissents of Justice Frankfurter in *Barnette* and Justice Black in *Tinker*, the *Hazelwood* majority insisted that "the education of the nation's youth is primarily the responsibility of parents, teachers, and state and local school officials, and not of federal judges" (273). Education, it seemed to assume, involves inculcative processes inconsistent with intellectual freedom and thus inconsistent with First Amendment protection. If we want the government to educate, we must not shackle it with the First Amendment.

Justice Brennan's dissent acknowledged that "the public educator's task . . . demands particularized and supremely subjective choices among diverse curricula, moral values, and political stances . . . and among various methodologies" (278). But, he added, although the court had "traditionally reserved the 'daily operation of school systems' to the states and their local school boards" (278–279), it had "not . . . hesitated to intervene where their decisions run afoul of the Constitution" (279, citing cases including *Meyer v. Nebraska* [1923] and *West Virginia v. Barnette* [1943]).

Justice Jackson, in *Barnette*, was well aware of the concern that the Supreme Court would become "'the school board for the country'" (637, quoting from *Minersville v. Gobitis* [1940]). He provided what remains, I think, the definitive response:

> Boards of Education have . . . important, delicate, and highly discretionary functions, but none that they may not perform within the limits of the Bill of Rights. That they are educating the young for citizenship is reason for scrupulous protection of constitutional freedoms of the individual, if we are not to strangle the free mind at its source and teach youth to discount important principles of our government as mere platitudes.
>
> Such boards are numerous and their territorial jurisdiction often small. But small and local authority may feel less sense of responsibility to the Constitution, and agencies of publicity may be less vigilant in calling it to account. . . .
>
> The very purpose of a Bill of Rights was to withdraw certain subjects from the vicissitudes of political controversy, to place them beyond the reach of majorities and officials and to establish them as legal principles to be applied by the courts. One's right to life, liberty, and property, to free speech, a free press, freedom of worship and assembly, and other fundamental rights may not be submitted

to vote; they depend on the outcome of no elections. (*West Virginia v. Barnette* 1943, 637–638)

Barnette, moreover, was not just about the First Amendment rights of individuals. Transcending the question of individual rights, it construed the First Amendment as a structural protection of democratic government. For public education to indoctrinate students not only violates their rights as individuals, and those of their parents, but also undermines the democratic ideal of government by the will of the governed. Academic freedom is "a special concern of the First Amendment" (*Keyishian* 1967, 603) because indoctrination is a special threat to democracy.

Keyishian's pronouncement that academic freedom is a special concern of the First Amendment has not been explicitly overruled, though it may today apply only to colleges and universities (if anywhere). It is not inconceivable that a strong right to nonindoctrination, founded on *Barnette*, could some day reemerge in American education law and limit the reach of *Hazelwood*. Even without a constitutional conception of academic freedom, First Amendment principles may someday be applied more systematically in various educational contexts, moving toward standards like those of *Tinker*. For the foreseeable future, however, although First Amendment principles provide useful guidance in conceptualizing intellectual freedom, judicial applications of the First Amendment will protect only limited aspects of academic freedom.

Even if the First Amendment were strictly applied, however, it would be a mistake to rely on First Amendment law to fully protect academic freedom. One obvious reason is that the First Amendment only restricts U.S. governmental (including state and local) authority. Even with regard to educational institutions subject to First Amendment constraints, however, there are at least three additional reasons not to rely on the First Amendment.

First, it is not clear that the First Amendment, even properly interpreted and strictly applied, encompasses and resolves all issues of intellectual freedom in public academic contexts. Education and research may require intellectual freedoms beyond those legally required even under an expansive interpretation of the First Amendment.

Second, at a practical level, even if courts were to vigorously apply the First Amendment to educational issues that come before them (and even if the First Amendment were theoretically adequate to fully protect academic freedom), most violations of intellectual freedom in public education would never get to court. Academic freedom should not depend on the willingness and ability of faculty and students to sue their schools and colleges.

Finally, aside from the practical and theoretical limitations of judicial oversight and the First Amendment, it is a mistake in principle to construe academic freedom as a set of restrictions imposed on educational institutions by authorities external to them. Courts may provide some protection against some violations of academic freedom, and U.S. courts should, in my view, provide much more protection than they do. In the end, however, academic freedom must arise from the internal commitments of academic communities to principles intrinsic to the nature and purpose of education and research. In the next chapter I propose, explain, and justify a set of five such principles.

Chapter 4
Principles of Academic Freedom

What is academic freedom, and why should educators, students, parents, citizens, and others be concerned with it? I have suggested that academic freedom is best construed not as a matter of special rights or final authority associated with particular persons, roles, or institutions, but rather as *intellectual freedom in educational and research contexts*. There are at least four interrelated reasons for a special concern with academic freedom. These may be labeled *educational*, *moral*, *democratic*, and *multicultural*.

First, higher levels of intellectual freedom enhance learning, development, and inquiry. We are more likely to make progress in understanding when we reflect, discuss, and inquire under conditions of intellectual freedom. In fact, intellectual freedom is a necessary condition for academic work because education and research require the freedom of students, teachers, and researchers to assess the justifiability of potential beliefs, apply diverse forms of reasoning, seek out what they deem to be relevant information, reach whatever conclusions seem most justifiable, and discuss their ideas with others. In the absence of intellectual freedom, genuine education and research are impossible.

Second, respect for students as persons entails a moral obligation not to use purportedly educational processes for the purpose of indoctrination. This is an obligation of teachers to their students and of administrators, board members, legislatures, and others to the educational institutions for which they are responsible. Learning without liberty is indoctrination, not education.

Third, public education in a democratic society must provide for the transmission of knowledge and values across generations without undermining the democratic ideal of government by the will of the governed. For democracy to continue, the next generation must develop a will of its own. Nonindoctrination protects not only the moral rights of individual students but also the moral and constitutional legitimacy of public education (*West Virginia v. Barnette* 1943; see Chapter 2).

Finally, intellectual freedom limits the possibility of some cultural factions using public education to indoctrinate the entire next generation in particular religious, philosophical, or other ultimate views. Democracy entails a commitment not to indoctrinate each other's children. Academic freedom is thus particularly important in safeguarding the democratic legitimacy of public education in a multicultural society.

It is not enough, however, to conclude that intellectual freedom is important and should therefore be highly valued. We must specify what it means to value intellectual freedom in educational and research contexts, and thus what academic freedom entails. In this chapter I propose a set of five principles that together provide a comprehensive and justifiable conception of academic freedom as intellectual freedom in educational and research contexts.

I do not propose this set of principles as the one true conceptualization of academic freedom. On the other hand, as noted in the preface, the present principles were not sketched on a party napkin two days before the manuscript for this book was due to the publisher. Their history goes back to the 1980s and their current formulation is the result of considering the application of an evolving set of principles to hundreds of cases over the past quarter-century. In the present chapter I present the five principles of academic freedom, including some preliminary explanation and justification. The true test of the principles, however, lies in their application to the cases in the remaining seven chapters.

1. Freedom of Belief and Identity

All persons, including students and teachers, have an ultimate right to believe and value whatever they believe and value, to maintain or change their beliefs and values as they choose, and to define themselves in terms of whatever beliefs and values they deem central to their identities. Educational institutions may present alternative views and values, but may not impose or require belief or commitment. Students may be evaluated and graded with regard to their understanding of and reasoning about curricular material but not on the basis of their agreement with particular viewpoints. Teachers and researchers may be evaluated on the basis of the quality of their teaching and research, but not on the basis of their viewpoints.

Freedom of speech is vital to intellectual freedom, and more generally to any defensible conception of human rights, but freedom of speech requires freedom of belief, which can thus be seen as the foundation of intellectual freedom. Without freedom of belief we have nothing to say, or at least no rational basis for deciding what to say. Indeed, freedom of any sort requires freedom of belief, without which we have no basis for deciding what to do. Freedom of belief includes the freedom to adopt, maintain, modify, or abandon diverse beliefs and values on the basis of our own evaluation of those beliefs and values, thus enabling us to act on the basis of reasons of our own, a minimal condition of rational agency. To the extent that the beliefs and values that guide us are imposed by others, we cannot function autonomously. Freedom of belief is thus a necessary condition for rational agency and autonomy, and therefore a fundamental right. To coerce, manipulate, or punish beliefs fails to respect individuals as persons.

Freedom of belief encompasses not only particular ideas but also comprehensive and ultimate doctrines, systems of belief that are central to identity. Even with respect to young children, education must not compromise the ability to form an identity of one's own. Identity formation is of course central to development in adolescence and early adulthood, and matters of identity remain fundamental throughout our lives. Students and faculty have an ultimate right to determine not only what they believe but who they are.

These principles are fully applicable to all values, ideas, ideologies, and identities—without exception. Freedom of belief is absolute.

2. Freedom of Expression and Discussion

All persons have a right to express their views and to discuss them with others. In academic contexts, students and teachers have a right to express their views on any matter relevant to the curriculum even if those views are deemed to be false, absurd, offensive, or otherwise objectionable. Evaluations of student and faculty work, and restrictions on the time, place, or manner of expression, must be neutral with respect to viewpoint. Special steps to avoid misunderstandings may be necessary when an individual is speaking in an official capacity on behalf of an educational institution or professional organization or is addressing an audi-

ence that may fail to distinguish the individual from the institution, organization, or discipline that she or he appears to represent.

Freedom of belief would have limited meaning and value if one's right to express one's beliefs could be made contingent on what one believes. Restrictions on expression must be viewpoint-neutral in order to respect the equal right of all persons, regardless of what they believe, to express their beliefs. The right to express one's beliefs must not be restricted simply because some persons or groups, or the community at large, object to those beliefs—no matter how strong or well justified those objections may be. Freedom of expression encompasses a right to participate in discussion on an equal basis with others regardless of one's point of view. Faculty must teach the content of the curriculum and students must learn it, but individual students and teachers have an absolute right to believe whatever they believe and to express those beliefs to the extent that they are relevant to the curriculum.

Evaluation of student and faculty work must be based on the content of that work, and thus cannot be content-neutral, but need not and must not be based on viewpoint. Student and faculty writing, for example, may be evaluated for quality of expression and argument, but not on the basis of whether the evaluator agrees with the conclusion reached. A teacher may receive a lower evaluation for being unable to explain ideas important to the curriculum but not for disagreeing with those ideas or presenting alternatives.

Similarly, the process of education requires restrictions on the time, place, and manner of expression, but such restrictions must be viewpoint-neutral. Students who wish to speak in class, for example, may be required to raise their hands and wait for acknowledgment from the teacher—but permission to speak must not be granted or withheld on the basis of viewpoint. Even content-based restrictions may be legitimate, provided they are not viewpoint-based. A teacher may restrict comments irrelevant to the current topic of discussion, for example, but must not restrict relevant ideas simply because they are objectionable.

Freedom of expression, then, is a fundamental right of all individuals, including students and teachers. But that's not all. Freedoms of expression and discussion are especially important in an academic context because they serve the academic purpose of promoting inquiry, learning, and development. Educators have both moral and pragmatic reasons to support and promote free expression and discussion.

Educational institutions and professional organizations may in some cases adopt viewpoints of their own and may express these viewpoints through spokespersons whose role is to speak on their behalf. Freedom of expression does not license spokespersons to misrepresent those they claim to represent. Senior administrators, in particular, often speak for their schools, school systems, colleges, or universities, and may be perceived as doing so regardless of their intent. With this in mind, it is legitimate to expect such administrators to anticipate and minimize misattributions.

Individual faculty and students are generally assumed to be speaking only as individuals unless they specifically present themselves as speaking for their school, college, or academic discipline. In some circumstances, however, individual speakers should anticipate and avoid audience perceptions that they are speaking for others. For example, teachers may be perceived by students as presenting an expert consensus on a topic. When they are presenting alternative or personal ideas, they should be clear about that. Similarly, elementary school teachers should recognize that young children may fail to distinguish the personal views of their teachers—on matters of religion or politics, for example—from official positions of their schools. Here again, academic freedom does not mean never having to watch what you say.

3. Freedom of Inquiry

Educational institutions should encourage students and faculty to pursue their own interests and ideas and should promote access to relevant sources of information. Inquiry must not be suppressed by restricting access to particular authors, topics, or viewpoints, or by hindering the formulation of objectionable conclusions.

Educational institutions may require that student research relate to the curriculum and that it meet justifiable standards of quality in order to receive academic credit. Similarly, faculty who are expected to conduct research may be evaluated on the quality of that research. Such constraints on inquiry are necessarily content-based, but they can and must be viewpoint-neutral. Restrictions on student and faculty research must not be motivated by an intent to suppress particular facts, ideas, perspectives, or sources. In general, students and faculty should be encouraged, regardless of their beliefs and viewpoints, to pursue what they regard as their most important intellectual projects.

Freedom of inquiry includes a right of access to information and ideas. The American Library Association has long recognized the special role of libraries, including school libraries, with respect to access and inquiry:

> Libraries should provide materials and information presenting all points of view on current and historical issues. Materials should not be proscribed or removed because of partisan or doctrinal disapproval.
>
> School library media professionals assume a leadership role in promoting the principles of intellectual freedom within the school by providing resources and services that create and sustain an atmosphere of free inquiry.

The American Library Association has long been clear, moreover, that librarians must not deny or abridge the right to use a library on account of age. Children's inquiry may be limited by their parents, but it is not the role of the librarian to serve as parent.

Freedom to conduct research has traditionally been construed as a special right of university faculty, critical to society's vital interest in the progress of knowledge. Broadly construed as autonomous inquiry, however, research is intrinsic to rational learning, which includes ongoing processes of seeking information and testing ideas. Thus research is not a domain of academic freedom distinct from education, the special province of a distinct group known as "researchers." Research, learning, and the development of rationality are interrelated aspects of education, subject to the same general principles of academic freedom. The research of a young student may be less likely to add to human knowledge than that of a professor, but it is at least as likely to promote the rationality of the researcher. All research is fully entitled to the protections of academic freedom.

4. Freedom from Indoctrination

Educators and educational institutions must not require or coerce students to modify their beliefs or values. Efforts to convince students to modify their beliefs or values must be academically justifiable.

Nonindoctrination is the moral and constitutional core of academic freedom. It is generally legitimate to try to convince students to modify their views provided there is a genuine academic justification for doing so. Even where efforts to convince are justifiable, however, educators should adhere to ethical standards of nonindoctrination.

Educational institutions should protect students from indoctrination via appropriate procedures and standards.

4a. Formulation of Curriculum

Curriculum must be determined by teachers and other professionals on the basis of academic considerations. It is a responsibility of administrators and governing boards to explain and support justifiable curricular decisions and to educate their constituencies about the educational importance of an inclusive curriculum and the critical role of respect for academic freedom.

An idealized conception of education for rationality might envision a curriculum that addresses all topics, raises all issues, presents students with all points of view on those topics and issues, examines all arguments for and against all of those viewpoints, permits unlimited discussion of and reflection on all those arguments and viewpoints, and encourages the application of all justifiable modes of reasoning.

The impracticality of such a view is obvious. There are far too many topics, issues, viewpoints, arguments, and modes of reasoning even to approximate this approach. Moreover, it may be the fully legitimate purpose of education to highlight particular topics, issues, viewpoints, arguments, or modes of reasoning. Pragmatic and pedagogical considerations require educators to make choices about what books to assign, what topics and issues to raise, what viewpoints and arguments to pursue, and what modes of reasoning to advocate.

Nonindoctrination does not require a viewpoint-neutral curriculum. It does require, however, that the formulation of curriculum be based on academic considerations. In some cases there are academic reasons to choose some viewpoints rather than others for inclusion in the curriculum—they are better supported by evidence, more relevant to a particular topic, or more understandable to students at a given developmental or educational level. Not all choices are academically legitimate, however. Curricular choices must not be motivated by a fixed commitment to promote particular ideas and values regardless of logic and evidence. In democratic public education, moreover, curriculum decisions must not be motivated by an intent to favor or disfavor particular religions, political parties, or ultimate doctrines.

No matter who makes curriculum decisions and no matter what process is used, there is no guarantee that such decisions will be made entirely on academic grounds. In general, curricular decisions are most likely to be made on academic grounds when they are made in the course of deliberative processes by teachers and other professionals with specific curriculum-related expertise under conditions where they are protected from coercive pressures such as threats to their jobs. It is a fundamental role of administrators and governing boards to support this process by insulating faculty and other academic decision makers from such coercion. Administrators and governing boards may and should reject faculty determinations that are patently nonacademic—such as decisions based on bribery, sexual favors, or secret political deals—but must not simply substitute their own judgments for those of faculty.

Nonindoctrination requires that, in case of disagreement among faculty and other experts, a more inclusive curriculum should generally prevail. Where there is genuine disagreement within a discipline, students should learn about the dispute itself, not just about the currently prevailing view. In any case where an academically justifiable curriculum has been adopted by an appropriate group of teachers and experts through an academically justifiable process, individual teachers have an obligation to present whatever information and ideas are included in the curriculum, even if they disagree with what they are presenting or doubt its importance to their students. Individual teachers may, however, supplement the curriculum by presenting additional information and ideas and by expressing and explaining their disagreement with aspects of the curriculum.

4b. Challenges to the Curriculum

Suggested modifications of the curriculum should not be accepted merely to resolve a complaint, but neither should such suggestions automatically be rejected as illegitimate. In general, changes that expand the curriculum are more likely to be defensible than changes that contract or restrict it. On the other hand, additions may be illegitimate if what is added cannot be justified academically, and deletions may be appropriate if what is deleted was not academically justifiable.

Faculty decisions about curriculum are not beyond question but must not be replaced with nonacademic decisions. Nonindoctrination entails a general disposition to favor inclusion over exclusion with regard to information and ideas in the curriculum. Challenges to the curriculum are more likely to be justifiable when they are motivated by an intent to add additional facts, ideas, perspectives, or sources than when they are motivated by an intent to suppress particular material. The ultimate criterion is whether the suggested change will enhance the opportunity of students to make justifiable decisions of their own about what to believe and what to do.

Challenges can often be resolved through individual accommodations that do not modify the curriculum for other students. As appropriate, students, parents, teachers, and schools should negotiate agreements that respect the rights of individual students, the educational authority of their parents, the education of other students, and the legitimate educational interests of the community.

5. Equality, Privacy, and Due Process

To the extent that violations of equal opportunity, privacy, and due process infringe on intellectual freedom in academic contexts, they are inconsistent with academic freedom.

Academic freedom refers primarily to intellectual freedom, but intellectual freedom is intrinsically connected to issues of equality, privacy, and due process.

5a. Equality

All students and faculty have an equal right to academic freedom.

All students and faculty have an equal right to academic freedom regardless of individual, biological, cultural, religious, theoretical, ideological, political, or other characteristics, backgrounds, or viewpoints.

Academic freedom does not entail—in fact is inconsistent with—a right to be shielded from beliefs and viewpoints one considers false, absurd, offensive, or otherwise objectionable. It does entail efforts to encourage all students to express their own views and participate in discussion. This may require special support for students who hold unpopular views or who are identified with demographic groups whose ideas and perspectives are not taken seriously by most students.

5b. Privacy

Educators and educational institutions must refrain from academically unjustified inquiries into the beliefs, values, interests, affiliations, and expressive activities of current and potential students and faculty and from academically unjustified uses of information about individuals' beliefs, values, interests, affiliations, and expressive activities.

Students may choose to speak, write, and reflect about their own beliefs, values, and viewpoints, and faculty may encourage them to do this for educational purposes. Intellectual freedom, however, includes a right not to discuss what one chooses to keep private and a right to have what one reveals for academic purposes kept within that academic context. Without such expectations of privacy, intellectual freedom is substantially constricted.

In admitting students, hiring faculty, and making decisions about current students and faculty, educational institutions should not seek out information about beliefs, values, interests, affiliations, or expressive activities except as these relate to the individual's academic competence and should not make use of academically irrelevant information about such matters.

5c. Due Process
Academic institutions must ensure that their formal and informal procedures provide sufficient due process to protect intellectual freedom.

Unpopular ideas and research projects may result in charges of subversion, treason, blasphemy, harassment, and so forth. Students and faculty with unpopular ideas will not feel free to express their views and pursue their interests, and thus to partake in academic freedom, unless they are confident that patently frivolous charges will be dismissed promptly and that all charges will be investigated with due regard for freedoms of belief and expression.

Conclusion

These five principles (collected in the Appendix) present academic freedom as intellectual freedom in educational and research contexts. The test of the principles is whether they provide consistent and intuitively satisfying resolutions to issues of intellectual freedom faced by teachers and students. In the remaining seven chapters, I apply the principles to a series of cases illustrating many of the most difficult and contentious educational issues of recent years.

Part Two

Academic Freedom in Practice

Chapter 5

Canon to the Right of Us, Canon to the Left: Literature, Selection, and Censorship

A re there some books so fundamental that you cannot be considered an educated person unless you have read them? If so, then these books should be a required part of the curriculum in any educational institution that wants its graduates to qualify as educated people. But what books, if any, meet this criterion? What books merit inclusion in the canon—the list of indispensable books?

More generally, who should decide what books to assign in literature classes and on what basis should such decisions be made? Is there a canonical list of great books from which curricula should be fashioned? Should literature classes be limited to great books? Is there a scholarly consensus regarding what books are great?

Efforts to address these questions generate competing claims that some ideas, perspectives, or voices have been included or excluded for nonacademic reasons. Discussion of such matters, moreover, may be poisoned by charges and countercharges about who is indoctrinating whom. Is there an academic way out of this morass, or must we simply resign ourselves to the fact that the recurrent canon wars are entirely and inevitably political?

Case 5–1 *You are a student in a literature course in which nearly all the assigned novels are written by European or Euro-American men. You wonder why the selection of authors is not more diverse but you are concerned that if you ask about this you may be perceived as questioning the authority or competence of the instructor and others responsible for the course. What should you do?*

If someone forbid you to read books by women, or systematically stripped the school library of all books by persons of African ancestry, you would have a strong and obvious basis for complaint. You could argue that authors in the forbidden category were being censored and that your own freedom of inquiry was being suppressed "by restricting access to particular authors" (Principle 3).

The choice of what books to assign in a literature class, however, raises issues of curriculum much more subtle than this. The number of novels a teacher can expect students to read in a particular course is only a tiny fraction of the number of published novels. Someone has to decide which novels to assign. It would be absurd to argue that all the unassigned authors and novels have been censored or that your freedom of inquiry has been suppressed by not requiring you to read every novel ever published.

Nevertheless, it is critical to academic freedom that curriculum "be determined by teachers and other professionals on the basis of academic considerations" (Principle 4a). You have a legitimate interest as a student in knowing who selected the books for this class and on what basis those decisions were made.

How you ought to proceed depends on a variety of factors. Suppose, for example, you are a public high school student in a required English class. Without questioning the authority or competence of the instructor, you could ask how books are selected in classes such as this.

It might turn out that all assigned novels must be selected from a list approved by the local or state school board. This could lead to an interesting class discussion about how the school board makes its literary decisions, whether it ought to have the authority to make such decisions, how much freedom teachers should have to decide what books to assign, whether books by some kinds of people have been improperly favored or disfavored in the selection process, whether the result of the process is that students are being indoctrinated, and so forth. It might turn out that your teacher shares your concerns, or at least sees the educational value of discussing matters of this sort.

Suppose instead that you are a student in an advanced elective class on, say, U.S. literature of the nineteenth century. It turns out your teacher personally chose the assigned novels and believes they are the greatest works of nineteenth century American literature. In response to questions about why the authors are almost all males of European ancestry, the instructor responds that, because of discrimination against women and racial minorities in the nineteenth century, the vast majority of published novels—including the great ones—were published by men of European ancestry. His course selections, he insists, simply reflect the political realities of the period under study.

There is much more that could be said here, but what you say and how you say it must depend on context. If the instructor seems threatened and you have reason to fear the consequences of pursuing this issue, you might reasonably decide that you have raised the issue you wanted to raise and are content to let the instructor proceed with his design for the course. Alternatively, in some contexts, you might decide to pursue the issue in some way (see Case 5–6). An instructor who respects academic freedom, I might add, would appreciate your questions (see Case 5–5) and might even encourage the class to discuss the metacurricular controversies that generate what reaches them as curriculum.

Case 5–2   *You are a student in a literature course in which most of the assigned novels are written by women or by men of non-European background. You wonder if some of these novels were included in the course not because of their intrinsic value but because of the demographic characteristics of their authors. You feel like you're being indoctrinated in multiculturalism and diversity, but you expect that your instructor and most of your fellow students will deem you racist or sexist if you question the selection of novels. What should you do?*

Although the politics of this case differs from the politics of Case 5–1, the underlying issue is identical. You should acknowledge the responsibility of your teacher and other experts to devise a curriculum and recognize that devising a curriculum entails choosing what books to include. At the same time, you have a right to know who devised the curriculum and on what basis and you have a right to question the process or results.

A question: What do you mean when you say you "feel like you're being indoctrinated in multiculturalism"? Is it that so many of the books in the course present cultural perspectives you've rarely encountered before? Being exposed to new perspectives, however, is central to education. This is not indoctrination even if you find some or all of the new perspectives useless, upsetting, or otherwise objectionable.

You do have a right, however, to question the value of what you are required to read and to encourage alternatives. If your questioning gets you censored or punished, then you are indeed being indoctrinated and you should appeal to higher authorities (see Case 5–6).

If your instructor respects academic freedom, however (see Case 5–5), your questions may enhance the quality of discussion and education in your class—to everyone's advantage.

Case 5–3   *Your child is a student in a course in which nearly all the assigned novels are written by European or Euro-American men. You wonder why the selection of authors is not more diverse but you are concerned that if you ask about this you may be perceived as questioning the authority or competence of the instructor and others responsible for the course, which could jeopardize your child. What should you do? Does this depend on the age of your child?*

Case 5–4   *Your child is a student in a literature course in which most of the assigned novels are written by women or by males of non-European background. You wonder if some of these novels were included in the course not because of their intrinsic value but because of the demographic characteristics of their authors. You fear that your child is being indoctrinated in multiculturalism, but you expect that school authorities will deem you to be racist or sexist if you question the selection of novels. What should you do?*

These cases parallel Cases 5–1 and 5–2, but take a parental perspective. If your child is an adult you might provide advice, but you would most likely leave the matter between your child and his or her college or university. For younger students, however, parents usually (and properly) have a more direct relation with the school.

As a parent, you have both a right and a responsibility to ensure for your child an "academically justifiable" curriculum that does not "require or coerce students to modify their beliefs or values" (Principle 4). Thus you have a right and responsibility to ensure a curriculum that is "determined by teachers and other professionals on the basis of academic considerations" (Principle 4a) and is not simply an instrument for indoctrinating your child.

You should keep in mind, however, that exposure to perspectives different from your own is an inevitable part of education and does not in itself constitute indoctrination. Don't be too quick to assume or charge indoctrination. First, find out more about the course, about what is really being assigned, read, and discussed—and why. In talking with the teacher about this, be clear that you are not questioning his or her authority to make academic decisions about curriculum. At least for now, you simply want to know more about what decisions have been made and how these will affect your child's education.

Knowing more about the course and about the rationale for the curriculum may resolve your concerns, or it may not. If you continue to have objections you might ask yourself just what you would like to see added or removed and make suggestions to the teacher. Keep in mind, however, that a literature teacher cannot simply assign any novel that any parent or student endorses or remove from the curriculum any novel that any parent or student finds objectionable. Even if you find the curriculum less than ideal, you are free to talk with your child about any or all of the assigned novels and to suggest additional readings.

If after careful consideration you remain convinced that the teacher or school is making selections on nonacademic grounds and thus indoctrinating your child, whether in mainstream or multicultural perspectives and values, you should consider bringing your complaint to an appropriate administrator. Of course, you will need to consider the likely implications of this for your child and may decide this is not a battle you wish to drag him or her into. On the other hand, children may understand and appreciate their parents' commitment to seeing that they are educated rather than indoctrinated. Older children and adolescents, moreover, may have opinions of their own.

Case 5–5   As the teacher of a literature course, you are approached by a student or parent who believes the course includes too few or too many female or minority authors. How should you respond?

First, you should clearly acknowledge the legitimacy of the query. Curriculum should be the result of academically justifiable decisions and it is part of your role as a teacher to explain and justify your teaching, especially if there are doubts or questions.

Nevertheless, although suggestions from students and parents should not "automatically be rejected as illegitimate," neither should suggested modifications "be accepted merely to resolve a complaint" (Principle 4b). In general, you should be more open to "changes that expand the curriculum" than to "changes that contract or restrict it" (Principle 4b). The bottom line is your responsibility to teach an academically justifiable curriculum.

In some cases you may be able to satisfy concerned parents or students without modifying the curriculum by permitting students to opt out of some books and add others. If you believe that a general modification of the curriculum is not feasible or not academically justifiable, this is an option you should seriously consider. There may be cases, however, where you sincerely believe that a student cannot meet the legitimate expectations of your course without reading certain books or that proposed alternative books "cannot be justified academically" (Principle 4b). What you do in a case like this may depend on personal and political factors such as your tenure status and expectation of administrative support. Norms of academic freedom suggest, however, that you have not only a right but a responsibility to maintain and defend the academic integrity of your course.

Case 5–6   *As a school administrator you are approached by students or parents who believe the literature curriculum is overly dominated by Euro-American and male authors. The next day you are approached by another set of students or parents who believe the school assigns too many works of literature by nontraditional authors. How should you respond?*
Your immediate response to anyone who questions the curriculum should be to acknowledge such questions as legitimate. You should be clear, however, that "curriculum must be determined by teachers and other professionals on the basis of academic considerations" (Principle 4a). You should ask whether the students or parents have discussed their concerns with the relevant teachers. If not, you should urge that such discussion is a necessary first step in addressing the issue.
If the appropriate teachers have been approached and have not made sufficient changes to satisfy the concerned students or parents, you must now decide on your own response. In general, unless you believe those responsible for the curriculum are incompetent or have acted unprofessionally, you should "explain and support" their decisions (Principle 4a). You should be clear that your support for your teachers is not based on an independent determination that they have made the right choices. Selection decisions are necessarily subjective. There is no right answer to the question of what proportion of assigned authors should fit in various demographic categories. But some decisions are more justifiable than others, and it is teachers and experts in literature who have the expertise to make the most justifi-

able decisions about the literature curriculum. You cannot simply substitute your judgment for the judgments of those with greater relevant expertise than you. Rather, your role is to see that these judgments are made by the appropriate individuals under the appropriate conditions.

There may be rare circumstances where you have reason to believe that curriculum decisions were not made by qualified individuals or were not made on academic grounds. Relatedly, you may believe that the curriculum as a whole is designed or delivered in such a way as to indoctrinate students rather than educate them. Even in these cases, you must not simply replace the judgments of teachers and other experts with your own. You may, however, choose to get further input from additional experts or set in motion a process of reconsideration by appropriate experts. The challenge for you as an administrator is to facilitate communication and decision making without taking direct responsibility for curricular decisions.

Case 5–7   *As an expert in U.S. literature, you have been appointed to a committee charged with preparing a list of great works of U.S. literature that all students in the United States should read before they graduate from high school. How would you suggest the committee proceed?*

Proceed with great caution, to say the least. For a centralized panel to determine the literature curriculum for every student in every school in the country would threaten the autonomy of local communities and of individual teachers and students. On the other hand, it would be too quick simply to reject centralized decision making as indoctrination. Curriculum decisions must be made, and local decision makers can also indoctrinate.

Your committee may play a useful role if it keeps its focus on inclusion. The problem with imposing a long list of books to be read by all students is that, regardless of how important these books may be, filling the curriculum with them limits the opportunity for local and individual decision makers to add books of local or individual interest. Relying entirely on local and individual decision making, however, can result in a narrow curriculum that omits many great books. Your committee may play a useful role if it provides a short list of required books to be supplemented by local and individual choices. Perhaps even better, your committee could provide a long and diverse list of recommended books with the understanding that local curriculum committees and individual teachers and students will choose some assignments from this list and add some choices of their own.

Before the committee begins naming books, then, it is important that it discuss its mandate and reach a shared understanding consistent with principles of academic freedom. Such principles neither require nor forbid a national curriculum committee but they do require that if there is to be such a committee it must consist of teachers and others with relevant expertise (Principle 4a) and its conclusions must not unduly constrain local and individual choices (Principle 3). With this in mind, the committee might then generate a substantial list of worthy books to be considered by those making curriculum decisions and, perhaps, a much shorter list of truly indispensable books that every student, or at least those in public schools, must read.

Case 5–8 *As a member of the elected governing board of a public school system, you are approached by constituents who believe the curriculum systematically endorses and promulgates a Euro-American or male worldview. The next day you are approached by another set of constituents who believe the school has become a center of multicultural indoctrination. How should you respond? Does it matter whether the constituents who approach you attend or have children in the school? Would it matter if you were a member of a state legislature rather than a governing board?*

As a member of an elected governing board, your proper relation to curriculum is much like that of an administrator. You are responsible in a general sense for the operations of your school system and this includes a responsibility to see that curriculum is formulated by qualified individuals on academic grounds and is not devised or implemented as a means to indoctrinate students. You have no legitimate authority to formulate or alter curriculum, however, and you should be clear about this with your constituents. You should advise them to discuss their concerns with relevant teachers and, if this fails to satisfy them, with appropriate administrators.

What if discussions with teachers and administrators fail to satisfy your constituents? Only if you conclude there is a serious problem should you step in. If, for example, it appears that teachers and administrators are united in assigning only works by Euro-American males, or only works by nontraditional authors, there may indeed be a genuine issue of indoctrination to be addressed. The proper solution to the problem, however, is not a vote by the governing board to add or delete particular books. Rather the governing board might appoint a committee of teachers and other experts to reconsider the curriculum on an appropriate academic basis.

In the present case, it is worth noting—and pointing out to your constituents—that the curriculum is under attack by both multiculturalists and traditionalists. This does not guarantee that it is perfectly balanced, whatever that might mean. It does suggest, however, that the challenged curriculum is not the result of a single-minded agenda to limit students to particular types of authors or to indoctrinate them in particular ideologies. Absent evidence of such violations of students' academic freedom, it would violate the academic freedom of both teachers and students for you to intervene.

What if the complaints come from individuals who neither attend nor have children in the school? This should not affect your reaction. All members of a community have a legitimate interest in the public schools of that community. You may not see a basis for taking action, but this conclusion should be based on the nature of the complaint, not on who is complaining.

What if the complaints come to you as a member of a state legislature? Here you are even further removed from legitimate curriculum decisions and should be even more hesitant to take direct action. You should direct complaints to teachers first, then to administrators, and then to the appropriate governing board. If there is a serious problem that cannot be resolved in this way, the legislature may need to reconsider the system of educational governance for which it has ultimate responsibility, but it should not usurp the authority of governing boards or make curriculum decisions of its own.

There is a political reality worth noting here. If the complaints that come to you as an elected member of a governing board or legislature have widespread support, and you are interested in reelection, you may be tempted to do whatever it takes to satisfy the largest number of potential voters. You should resist this temptation. Academic freedom is not always popular, but it is a fundamental condition for a defensible system of education. Governance and politics require compromises, but academic freedom is one of those things that should not be compromised. Those responsible for a system of education have an obligation "to explain and support justifiable curricular decisions and to educate their constituencies about the educational importance of an inclusive curriculum and the critical role of respect for academic freedom" (Principle 4a).

Case 5–9   *After a shocking and highly publicized act of violence in your community, your principal sends a memo to all teachers that the school curriculum—including all assigned readings—must be responsive and responsible. Endorsement or advocacy of violence are strictly forbidden. As a high school English teacher, what should you do?*

It is certainly understandable that your principal doesn't want his school to be seen as endorsing or advocating violence, especially at a time when this has become a matter of acute community concern. The memo, however, is a severe restriction on academic freedom and seriously threatens the quality of education. It is a special threat, ironically, to your ability to educate students about violence. You should join with other teachers in an effort to convince the principal to reconsider.

Violence is a pervasive part of life and a major theme of literature. To forbid assigning any work that includes violent behaviors, persons, or events would be, in effect, to ban most classic and contemporary stories and novels—not to mention texts and other writings in history, psychology, sociology, and other fields. Your principal apparently recognized this and worded the memo so that it does not ban all mention of violence but rather focuses on endorsement and advocacy of violence.

This is still a broad ban on important educational materials, however. Must we exclude any book in which a character feels justified in harming another? What if someone in the book endorses physical self-defense? What if a character in the book endorses the death penalty? What if someone advocates going to war? Does it matter if the book as a whole questions or opposes the endorsement of violence within it?

Even if the ban were limited to books that clearly and directly endorse or advocate violence, that still would be highly restrictive. Will we ban any book that calls for war? What about books that defend or glorify past wars? Will we ban any book that endorses violent self-defense or advocates the death penalty? What about books that advocate spanking children? Many books endorse or advocate some kinds of violence under some circumstances. And come to think of it, with the exception of a small number of consistent pacifists, don't we all?

Rather than forbid endorsement or advocacy of violence, we should recognize that the study of literature provides an excellent context for consideration of violence. Readings should expose students to multiple examples of violence. Teachers should actively encourage reflection and discussion, which may involve forays into history, sociology, anthropology, psychology, biology, and other fields where violence is observed and studied.

But what if the readings themselves cause violence? This underlying fear is rooted in a simplistic psychological assumption that stimuli cause behaviors much as a billiard ball hitting another billiard ball causes it to move. This mechanistic conception of causality is fine for billiard balls but fails to account for complex biological and psychological systems and processes. Cognitive, developmental, and educational psychologists have long recognized that we assimilate what we encounter, including what we read, to prior knowledge and values. The challenge for teachers is to encourage and foster productive ways of thinking about the human propensity for violence. We cannot keep violence out of students' minds, but we can teach about violence and encourage moral development (see also Case 10–6).

What if the principal stands by the memo? You could appeal to a higher administrator or to the school board. You could also appeal to public opinion. In either case, you should be aware that the principal's memo probably will seem sensible, and even necessary, to most people. You are most likely to succeed if the case against the memo is brought by a broad coalition of teachers representing a variety of fields who can point to specific books that would be banned under the memo and explain why those books are valuable to education, including education about violence. It will also help if you can identify professional organizations to support your appeal.

What if you are unsuccessful in getting the memo rescinded? You may decide to avoid books that could lead to trouble. That would be understandable, but if many teachers make that decision the curriculum will be much impoverished. This will not make students less violent. On the contrary, it will deprive them of important opportunities to read, think, and talk about violence.

With that in mind you may decide to test the limits of the memo or even to assign books that clearly violate it. Obviously you should weigh the personal risks of such action against the educational bene-fits. If you do go ahead you should make sure that, in case of a chal-lenge, you know exactly why you have assigned the books in question and can explain and justify those decisions on educational grounds.

Case 5–10   *In addition to teaching literature you have long been an activist for social justice. Over the years, as this has become an increas-ingly important part of your life, you have increasingly assigned novels that focus on social and political issues in contemporary society. In dis-cussing these novels, you highlight the need for cultural transformation. Many students appreciate the readings and discussion but others com-plain that your course is political rather than educational. How should you respond?*

In identifying novels to assign to your students you should con-sider factors such as their literary quality, historical or contemporary significance, and accessibility to your students. In most cases, that will leave many excellent choices, more than you can assign. Having a theme may help you choose among the remaining options and may be educationally beneficial to your students.

In selecting a theme, however, it is important to recall that your students are in your class to learn about literature, not to learn about whatever happens to interest you, and certainly not to be indoctri-nated in your political or religious views. Your obligation not to indoctrinate your students forbids you to take advantage of having a captive audience that is required to read what you assign (see also Case 10–9).

Is social justice a reasonable theme? It could be, but much depends on what you mean by social justice and how you approach it. Social justice can be taken to mean respect for general principles of liberty, privacy, equality, and due process such as those found in the U.S. Con-stitution and the Universal Declaration of Human Rights. If your theme of social justice means that several of the books assigned in your course relate to civil liberties questions such as these, that does not in itself constitute indoctrination, even if the books raise questions that some would deem political. If, on the other hand, the books are chosen to systematically advocate a particular position on a current political con-troversy, that does seem to go over the line to indoctrination—even if most students agree with the position advocated.

Where exactly is the line between education and indoctrination in a case like this? That is not entirely clear, but you should make sure to stay well short of indoctrination. One way to do so is to be clear with your students that social justice is a complex concept, not a simple rule, which is what makes it worth studying. What is social justice? The readings you assign should raise this question, not assume and impose your own answer to it.

As for cultural transformation, you should be clear with your students (and with yourself) that not all transformations represent progress. Cultural transformation is not necessarily a good thing, and there may be disagreement about the value and consequences of any particular transformation. You can assign readings that raise issues of cultural transformation but you are indoctrinating your students if you select those readings with the intent of limiting them to a particular view of cultural transformation.

What is central here is genuine respect for your students, whether or not any of them complain. Your interests, values, and personal commitments will inevitably influence your choice of what your students read but you have an obligation to make those choices with the best interests of your students in mind. It may be in your students' best interest to be exposed to issues you deem especially important but it is not in their best interest to be indoctrinated in your specific views. In assigning books that address controversial political and social issues, you should be especially careful of this distinction.

Chapter 6
Apes and Evolutionists: Biology and Ideology

We now turn from literature to science. The most significant religious and political controversy related to science education, at least in the United States, has been the ongoing evolution/ creation dispute, involving profound disagreements about what should be taught concerning the age of the earth and the origin and evolution of living things. Many Christians deem scientific accounts of these matters contrary to the biblical account of creation. This controversy was a focus of national attention in 1925 due to the highly publicized trial of John Scopes, who was convicted of teaching students about evolution in violation of Tennessee law. The teaching of evolution remained illegal in many states for the next several decades. Even in states without antievolution laws, the topic of evolution was generally deemed too controversial to address in schools.

In the 1960s, however, as part of a national effort to enhance science education, biology courses increasingly included evolution, in some cases as a major part of the curriculum. In Arkansas, where the teaching of evolution was illegal, the inclusion of evolution led to a lawsuit that ultimately reached the U.S. Supreme Court. In *Epperson v. Arkansas* (1968), the court ruled that antievolution laws in Arkansas and other states served no purpose other than to support Christianity and thus constituted an establishment of religion in violation of the First Amendment.

Recognizing that the teaching of evolution could no longer be banned, critics of evolutionary theory devised an alternative strategy of requiring a balanced approach that gives equal time to creationist views. Such an approach, however, faced the constitutional problem that creationism is a religious doctrine. The solution was to strip the creationist view of all religious references and claim that what remained was a scientific theory. The result was *scientific creationism*, a theory that parallels biblical creationism in all respects except that it omits all mention of God or supernatural causation. Laws mandating so-called balanced treatment of evolution and scientific creationism, however, were struck down by federal courts, which concluded that scientific creationism had no scientific basis. In *Edwards v. Aguillard* (1987), involving an appeal of a Louisiana law, the U.S. Supreme Court agreed that the sole purpose of the Louisiana legislature was to promote Christianity. In the absence of any scientific basis for creationism, the legislature's claim that its purpose was to protect academic freedom through "balanced treatment" was deemed a sham.

Forced to adapt to a hostile constitutional environment, creationism continued to evolve. Its next instantiation was *intelligent design*, a doctrine claiming that some biological systems are so "irreducibly complex" that they could not have evolved from simpler systems through a process of natural selection and thus could only be the product of an intelligent designer. Although the intelligent designer was not identified as God, intelligent design was found by a federal court in *Kitzmiller v. Dover* (2005) to be no more scientific than earlier versions of creationism and thus equally indefensible as a mandated part of the science curriculum.

The controversy continues unabated, however. Questions about the emergence of life and humanity, no less than those concerning multiculturalism and literature, cut to the heart of our diverse ideologies and identities. A careful look at specific cases, however, suggests that in science, as in literature, curricular controversies can be resolved in a manner consistent with educational excellence and individual rights by applying principles of academic freedom. Questions about what should be taught in science classes (and how) should be addressed on the basis of general principles concerning who should determine curriculum, and on what basis, and associated principles concerning the rights and interests of students, parents, and communities.

Case 6–1   *You are a student who has been taught all her life that God created the earth about six thousand years ago and at that time created all species in their current forms. Now you are taught in science classes that the earth is billions of years old and that species evolve over thousands of generations. Can you be required to take these classes? Can you be required to take exams in these classes? Can you be required to renounce your views or to agree to alternative views?*

First of all, it is important to be clear that you have an absolute right to believe whatever you believe. This does not imply or assume that your beliefs are correct, or even that they might turn out to be correct. Even if your beliefs are demonstrably wrong, you have a right to believe what you believe, and nobody can require that you change your beliefs (Principle 1).

Your school, however, could not function if it were forbidden to present any idea contrary to the view of any student. Provided your school does not "impose or require belief or commitment," it "may present alternative views and values" (Principle 1). No one may deliberately undermine your religious beliefs by requiring you to take a course you find religiously objectionable simply because you find it religiously objectionable (Principle 4). If appropriate authorities have determined on academic grounds that a particular course is a necessary requirement, however, you must take the course. For example, it may reasonably be decided that a year of biology, or a course that addresses the age of the earth, is necessary for a high school diploma.

Thus, you do not have a right to avoid exposure to ideas you find objectionable, even if those ideas are objectionable with regard to your most fundamental beliefs and commitments. In fact, given that passing a class normally requires you to demonstrate your understanding of the material, you can be required to take exams and meet other requirements intended to assess your understanding of course material—including those ideas you find objectionable.

Understanding is not the same as belief, however. "Students may be evaluated and graded with regard to their understanding of and reasoning about curricular material but not on the basis of their agreement with particular viewpoints" (Principle 1). Thus your instructor may expect you to know that geologists believe the earth to be billions of years old and to be able to state what geologists take to be the evidence and arguments that support this view. Your instructor may not require you to find the geological evidence and arguments convincing, however. An exam devised to respect academic freedom would permit you to show what you know and how well you can reason without requiring you to adopt any particular point of view.

Case 6–2   *You are the parent of the student in Case 6–1. Should you complain to the school? What is your complaint? Does the age or educational level of the student matter?*

Provided the school is educating rather than indoctrinating your child, you have little to fear. Children interpret what they learn in school by assimilating it to the beliefs and values they bring from home. This is not to say that you can insulate them against new information or viewpoints but you can be confident they will not simply replace what you have taught with what they learn in school. Rather they will construct a series of understandings that reflect their ongoing efforts to coordinate multiple ideas.

If the school is indoctrinating your child, however, it may undermine the constructive efforts of your child's own mind—an infringement on his or her rights and yours. Some questions to ask yourself, then, are the following: Is your child free to express her own beliefs? Does she feel humiliated for her beliefs or pressured to change them? Can she do well in this course or unit without betraying her convictions? Keep in mind that being exposed to an idea and being expected to understand it are not the same as being required to believe in it. Keep in mind that it is scientists and science teachers who should determine the science curriculum, not you. With these considerations in mind, if you still feel your child is being indoctrinated you should arrange to talk with the teacher.

How you proceed from here depends on this conversation and its results. The teacher may have no ill intent and may successfully reassure you and your child of his respect for her right to believe what she believes. The teacher may make changes in his instruction or exams that show more respect for freedom of belief. There is an excellent chance that a meeting with the teacher will alleviate your concerns.

On the other hand, you may come away convinced that the teacher is hostile to your family's religious beliefs and really is attempting to indoctrinate or humiliate your child. In this case, you should go to an administrator for assistance—with the possibility of further appeals within and outside the school system. The challenge for you as a parent is making good judgments as to whether you are fighting genuine indoctrination or simply exposure to objectionable ideas.

If your child has independent views on these matters, such views should also be respected. In fact, if your child is mature enough to have independent views on these matters, there may be no need for you to intervene on her behalf. She may be able, with your advice and support, to stand up for her own rights.

Case 6-3 *You are the teacher of the student in Case 6-1. How should you respond to a request from the student or parent to delete the topic of origins from your course or to give equal time to a creationist view? What if this request (or order) comes from an administrator, a governing board, a state legislature, or a curriculum committee?*

First, acknowledging that it is legitimate to question the curriculum (Principle 4b), you should listen carefully to the complaint and make sure you understand exactly what you are being asked to do. It may turn out, perhaps after some discussion and clarification, that the central concern is the student's right to hold and express creationist ideas or your respect for the religious beliefs of the family. You may resolve the problem by providing assurance of your respect for freedoms of belief and expression and by conducting your class in accord with Principles 1 and 2.

If this does not suffice, however, you should not modify the curriculum simply to resolve the complaint (Principle 4b). You should not delete the topic of origins simply because some (or even all) students or parents find it objectionable. Even the addition of creationist ideas, which may seem less objectionable than the deletion of evolutionary ideas, is illegitimate if you believe that the inclusion of these ideas "cannot be justified academically" (Principle 4b).

You are, however, free to make modifications that you consider academically legitimate. If there are creationist ideas that you deem scientifically plausible or useful you may present such ideas and related evidence and arguments to students. Even if you think creationism has no scientific basis whatsoever, you might decide there is a role for creationist ideas in a unit on the cultural context of science or on the relation of science to religion.

If you decline to make some or all of the requested changes, you need not and should not claim that you or other experts know the full and final truth about the matters in question. Expert claims to authority over the curriculum are not based on a presumption of infallibility. Emphasize that a decision not to include creationist views in the curriculum does not exclude the introduction and discussion of such views by students (Principle 2).

Your obligation to all your students may sometimes require you to make or support curricular decisions that some of them (or their parents) disagree with. To add to your problems, you may also be subject to pressure from other sources. In many aspects of your job you are properly subject to the will of administrators, governing boards, or even your state legislature. On matters of curriculum, however, you should resist nonacademic pressures, and this includes directives from administrators, governing boards, or legislatures to omit particular topics or ideas or to include them for nonacademic reasons.

Resisting political and religious pressures is easier said than done, of course, and there may be situations where you feel you have no choice but to compromise. You should keep in mind, however, your obligation to defend the right of your students to a curriculum devised on academic grounds. You should remind administrators and governing boards that their general responsibility for the quality of education within their jurisdiction is not a mandate to set curriculum but, on the contrary, a mandate "to explain and support justifiable curricular decisions" made by those authorized to make such decisions (Principle 4a). In the extreme, you may decide to violate illegitimate directives and laws because they undermine your responsibility to your students.

This is not to say, however, that you have absolute authority over your curriculum. If a properly constituted and properly functioning curriculum committee decides that your course must include certain creationist ideas, you have an obligation to present those ideas to your students. Even in this case, however, you have a right to criticize the ideas you are presenting and to present and justify alternative views (Principle 2).

Case 6–4   *You are the school administrator hearing the complaint of the parent in Case 6–2. How should you respond to a request for deletion of the topic of origins or equal time for a creationist view?*

First, you should see if the parent has talked with the teacher. If not, urge that such a meeting be the first step. Be clear that you regard the matter seriously, want to know how the meeting with the teacher turns out, and will take further action if appropriate.

Suppose the parent has talked with the teacher and is not satisfied. You should be clear that the science curriculum is formulated by science teachers and scientists and that it would violate standards of academic freedom for you to interfere with the curriculum (Principle 4a). At the same time, however, you are responsible for the academic freedom of students, including the right of students to hold and express creationist ideas (Principles 1 and 2).

With these considerations in mind, you will need to gather facts to determine what to do. If it turns out that the teacher is operating on the basis of justifiable curricular decisions and is fully respecting the academic freedoms of all students, you must decline to intervene further and should explain why such intervention would undermine education. If, on the other hand, you think the instructor is presenting as science a curriculum shaped by religious doctrines or is censoring student expression of ideas contrary to the curriculum, you must protect the right of students to a scientifically justifiable science curriculum presented in an environment of intellectual freedom.

Even if you conclude that there is no problem with the curriculum or the manner of instruction, you may nevertheless explore with the student, parent, and teacher possibilities for opting out of what the student or family may deem to be an objectionable educational experience. This is not always an option, however, and should not be permitted simply to defuse controversy. The authority of teachers and other professionals over curriculum includes the authority to determine what units are necessary to particular courses and what courses to particular diplomas, certifications, and degrees. You may suggest options to students and parents, but should keep these options within the bounds of what those with relevant expertise consider academically legitimate.

Case 6–5   *You are a member of the governing board to which the student in Case 6–1 or the parent in Case 6–2 complains after administrators uphold a faculty decision to maintain the present curriculum and require the full participation of the student.*

As a member of a governing board you have no more authority than an administrator over curriculum and should be clear about this with yourself and with anyone who complains to you. Your proper role in response to a complaint from a student or parent, or for that matter a concerned citizen, is to ensure that the school system for which you are responsible is engaged in education, not indoctrination, and is respecting the rights of all concerned (Principle 4).

Suppose, for example, it is alleged that a teacher is deliberately humiliating Christian students because of hostility to their religious beliefs and that administrators made no effort to look into this problem. In that case your board has a responsibility to determine if administrators responded seriously and appropriately to the complaint and, if not, whether the teacher is indeed violating the right of students to equal educational opportunity, including their right to exercise their own academic freedom regardless of their religious beliefs (Principle 5a). If, on the other hand, administrators have taken the complaint seriously and determined that the curriculum is scientifically defensible and is being taught in a manner fully consistent with academic freedom, then you must ratify the administrative decision regardless of your personal opinions about what should or should not be taught in this class.

There remains the question of exempting the student from some aspect of the curriculum. If this has not been seriously considered, it should be. It is not for you to make a final decision about this, however. Exemptions and alternative assignments are appropriate only when they maintain the academic integrity of the curriculum for each student. If scientists believe that some knowledge of evolution is necessary to pass a course in biology, you have no legitimate authority to reverse this judgment.

If an exemption has been granted, you may be tempted to dismiss any further challenge as moot. This would be too quick, however. If there is a remaining problem that has not been solved, you have an obligation to the other students in the class and the school. Nevertheless, you should be especially careful about intervening if no one else is complaining. Look for broader and continuing issues, but don't get drawn into a personal vendetta.

Case 6–6   *You are a member of the school board to which the teacher in Case 6–3 complains after the administration rules that the teacher must give equal time to creationist and evolutionist viewpoints. What should the governing board do? What if the administration has instead decided to exempt creationist students from this aspect of the curriculum? What if the administrative mandate is to respect the views of creationist students?*

Regardless of your personal views on this matter, your responsibility as a member of a governing board is to defend the integrity of the science curriculum and the academic freedom of teachers and students (Principle 4a). Any administrator who requires or forbids the teaching of particular ideas in particular classes is overstepping his or her authority. Your board has a responsibility to restrict overzealous administrators who intrude on the curriculum.

If administrators have instead exempted creationist students from aspects of the curriculum they find religiously objectionable you should keep in mind that this decision may be the result of a sincere effort to find a compromise that satisfies individual students and parents without modifying the curriculum for other students. This does not mean you should reject the teacher's complaint, however. The teacher is responsible for maintaining educational standards for all students, including those who object to what they are expected to learn. The board should only uphold exemptions that those responsible for the curriculum deem to be consistent with maintaining appropriate academic standards.

Finally, if the teacher is challenging an administrative mandate to respect the views of creationist students, you should determine exactly what administrators intended and what the teacher finds objectionable. If the administration meant to require the teacher to acknowledge the scientific legitimacy of creationist views, or even just to refrain from challenging such views, this is a serious infringement on the teacher's freedom of expression (Principle 2). Teachers "must not require or coerce students to modify their beliefs" but academically justifiable efforts "to convince students to modify their beliefs" by providing relevant evidence and arguments are fully legitimate and must not be restricted (Principle 4).

If, on the other hand, the administration merely meant to require the teacher to permit creationist students to express and defend their views and to refrain from responses intended to ridicule such students, this is a fully appropriate defense of students' academic freedom. In this case, the board should support the administration.

Case 6–7   *You are a member of a governing board responsible for a school system in which there has been considerable turmoil about the teaching of evolution. Would you support a motion to require the teaching of creationism? To forbid it? To require the teaching of evolution? To forbid it? To require balanced treatment of both? What if you are a state legislator and this is a proposed law? What if you are a citizen and this is an initiative on the ballot?*

First of all, your opinions about evolution, creation, and related matters should not enter into this. Your role is to "support justifiable curricular decisions" (Principle 4a). A board-initiated motion to require or forbid the teaching of creation or evolution in science classes would be a serious infringement on the right of students to a curriculum formulated by science teachers and scientists, not by boards of education.

It might be thought that a motion to require balanced treatment of evolutionist and creationist viewpoints acknowledges "the educational importance of an inclusive curriculum" (Principle 4a) and thus furthers academic freedom. This analysis assumes, however, that every issue has two sides. The reality is that there is a scientific consensus with regard to many questions and that, where controversy exists, there are often three or more sides, not just two. Sometimes there are two major viewpoints that have roughly equal scientific support and merit balanced treatment. But often this is not the case. Judgments about what viewpoints have sufficient scientific support and educational value to merit inclusion in the curriculum, and how to allocate attention among them, should be made by scientists and science teachers—not by elected or appointed officials.

Governing boards are responsible for the formulation and implementation of a school system's general goals and policies. Such matters cannot be addressed without raising issues of curriculum. A decision to put more emphasis on science education, for example, will have major implications—in a general sense—for the science curriculum. The challenge for the board is to recognize when it is moving over the line to address what topics, ideas, theories, and data should or should not be presented within the science curriculum— and to recognize the danger to academic freedom of stepping over this line.

State legislatures also have oversight over education, but only in an even more general sense than governing boards. State legislatures, moreover, are even more political than governing boards, and should recognize how political they are and how dangerous their influence must inevitably be for academic freedom. As a state legislator, you should oppose any law that would require or forbid teaching evolution or creation or require balancing of any sort.

As noted in the introduction to this chapter, the U.S. Supreme Court has struck down laws forbidding the teaching of evolution (*Epperson v. Arkansas* 1968) or requiring equal time for creationism (*Edwards v. Aguillard* 1987). The rationale in each case was that the motivation for the law was religious, rather than secular, and thus violated the First Amendment ban on the establishment of religion. The present analysis goes beyond this, suggesting that legislative meddling in curriculum is an offense to academic freedom regardless of whether it is religiously motivated.

Consider finally a ballot initiative that enables citizens to vote on whether evolution or creation should be taught or banned. This might seem a democratic process, but it is no more legitimate than a popular vote on whether an alleged criminal is guilty or innocent or on what medical treatments should be used for what diseases in a public hospital. Decisions about the guilt of a criminal must be made by a jury that has been presented with the relevant evidence and legal criteria and has deliberated until reaching a consensus. Decisions about medical treatment should be made by those directly concerned on the basis of expert medical advice.

Democracy does not entail majority control over all decisions, and curriculum decisions are among those that require special expertise and special protection from political and religious pressures. Citizens who respect academic freedom will resist any invitation to impose curricular mandates on teachers and students, even when they believe in the truth and importance of the ideas to be taught or in the falsity and danger of the ideas to be banned.

Case 6–8   *The legislature of your state has passed a law that all teaching of or about biological evolution and the age of the earth include a disclaimer informing students that evolution is a theory and that they are free to believe what they choose. What should you do as a teacher of biology, geology, or related sciences?*

A legislatively derived science curriculum is most fundamentally a violation of the right of students to a science curriculum founded on scientific considerations. It is also objectionable, however, in potentially forcing teachers to choose between their responsibility to the law and their responsibility to their students. Science teachers have good reason to oppose the passage of laws that restrict their and their students' academic freedom and to support the repeal of such laws.

Suppose despite your best efforts a law was passed and remained in place that required you to tell your students that the earth is no more than ten thousand years old and that species remain eternally fixed across generations, assertions that you believe to be clearly contrary to extensive scientific evidence. Your professional responsibility to your students, in this case, would require you to violate this law. If your job were at stake and you did not expect administrative support you might reasonably decide for personal reasons that you must follow the law, but you would be violating your educational and moral responsibility to your students by teaching them as truth what you believe to be false. And you would be rightly upset with the legislature for putting you in this position.

In the present case, however, the law simply requires you to present evolution as a theory and respect students' freedom to maintain creationist beliefs. Even if the law is ill advised, there may be options consistent with both the law and your responsibility to your students.

Consider first the mandate to inform your students that evolution is a theory. You may be aware of what you deem to be evolutionary facts, evidence of populations changing over generations. An evolutionary account of the origin of species, however, goes beyond specific facts in order to integrate and explain diverse findings. Thus there is, in a sense, a theory of evolution—or perhaps more accurately there are multiple theories of evolution. It is not a violation of scientific or educational integrity to tell students about the theoretical status of evolution.

What then is the problem? There are, I suggest, two problems with simply telling students that evolution is a theory. First, in ordinary discourse, a theory is simply a speculation—something yet to be confirmed. In science, by contrast, theories are general structures of explanation, central to all scientific understanding. Some theories are better established than others but theories are never proven true and thus transformed into facts. To call evolution a theory is not to disparage it in any way. The problem is that students may not understand this. Fortunately, in directing that you call evolution a theory, the legislature did not forbid you to explain what you mean by a theory and why theories are crucial to science. You can explain the theoretical status of evolution to your students in a manner that both follows the law and is scientifically respectable. First problem solved.

The remaining problem is that, regardless of what you say about theories, a special focus on the theoretical status of evolution may misleadingly imply to students that the theory of evolution is somehow more problematic than other scientific theories. But the legislature did not forbid you to address the theoretical status of other theories. Rather than single out evolution, you can teach students about scientific theories in general and provide a variety of examples—including but not limited to evolution.

Consider now the mandate to inform students that they are free to believe whatever they choose about matters of evolution and the age of the earth. Students are indeed free to believe whatever they choose about these matters. Informing them of their rights is not only reasonable but highly desirable. The problem here is not the requirement that you respect students' freedom of belief but the focus on evolution, with the implication that freedom of belief is irrelevant to other areas of science, where the truth is beyond question. The solution is to inform students that they have a right to formulate and maintain their own beliefs about everything (Principle 1). You can remind them of this when the curriculum turns to questions of evolution, thus complying with the law, but also remind them of the generality of their right to freedom of belief.

For the most part, these considerations apply regardless of the age or educational level of the students. What you teach and how you teach about evolution will vary across levels of education and particular courses, but with a little creativity you can probably follow the law in question in any class without compromising the scientific and educational integrity of the course. In some classes, moreover, you might directly call attention to the law and your response to it as part of a discussion of the social and cultural contexts of science and education.

Case 6–9   *A student in your biology course objects to your discussion of evolution by natural selection by noting that not all phenomena are the result of natural processes. An objective observer encountering Mount Rushmore, he argues, would reject the highly implausible theory that the likenesses of four presidents are the result of natural processes of erosion and would conclude instead that these likenesses are the result of intelligent design. Intelligent design, then, is not just a legitimate scientific approach but is in fact the correct explanation in this case and others. To reject it out of hand, he concludes, is unscientific.*

You may be tempted to dismiss this proposal out of hand by insisting that intelligent design is not science and should not be discussed in a biology class. But this will just reinforce the student's conviction that evolution is a pseudoscience unable to withstand scientific debate. Other students may also conclude that scientists refuse to discuss intelligent design because they cannot refute it.

A better approach might be to acknowledge the example as an interesting one and use it to consider the nature of science. The student is right, you might note, that many things (including Mount Rushmore) are the result of intelligent design. But in the case of Mount Rushmore we don't posit an intelligent designer who cannot be known. We know (or can find out) who sculpted the four presidents and how. Intelligent design is part of science when we can engage in research to identify and explain the intelligent designer. It is not part of science when the invocation of the designer ends the explanatory process, as when critics of evolution claim that a complex biological structure such as the eyeball cannot be the result of any natural process and must therefore have been created by an intelligent designer (but never mind who or how).

You may want to make clear that your intent in ruling out supernatural explanations is not to patrol the borders of what may be said in your classroom. Your students are free to say what they believe about apes, evolutionists, and the origin of species, and so are you (Principle 2). But the curriculum should be determined by scientists and educators on the basis of scientific and educational considerations (Principle 4a). Part of the curriculum in any field of science will consist of scientific findings. Questions about intelligent design, however, are a useful reminder that students also need to learn about the nature and methods of science.

Chapter 7

"Don't Know Much About History": Genocide, Denial, and Indoctrination

History texts, especially at the elementary and secondary levels, are designed and intended to be read as definitive summaries of what is known about the past, and are for the most part accepted by students as authoritative. More generally, history curricula are deemed to transmit knowledge of the past from those who have it (historians and teachers) to those who need it (students). Whoever controls the curriculum, then, to a large degree determines what the next generation believes about its history.

It is thus no surprise to find that, all over the world, the study of history is largely designed to foster nationalism, commitment to mainstream ideologies, and support for governmental policies. Antagonistic nations and groups may maintain their antagonism across generations in part due to the divergent histories they teach in their respective schools. Where dual (or multiple) historical narratives compete for control of a single educational system, controversy is likely to be intense. Each side pushes for what it sees as the objective truths of history—its own. Curriculum decisions may be distorted by political pressures.

In Sam Cooke's song "Wonderful World," a love-struck student cheerily admits that he doesn't know much about history because he hasn't been paying attention in class. Given the indoctrinative nature of most history curricula, there may be at least as much reason to worry about those students who do pay attention. What should students be taught about history? Who should make these decisions, and on what basis? What are the rights and interests of students, parents, and communities in this regard?

Case 7–1   As a history teacher covering a unit on World War II, you discuss the Holocaust, which you define as the Nazi effort to exterminate Jews and Gypsies. A student suggests that the Nazi campaign against Gypsies was not genocidal and thus not part of the Holocaust. Another student argues, to the contrary, that not only did the Nazis commit genocide against Jews and Gypsies but the Holocaust also included exterminations of Poles, homosexuals, Jehovah's Witnesses, the disabled, and others. A third student responds that many people from many backgrounds died in World War II but there was no specific Nazi effort to exterminate particular groups. A fourth student adds that the Holocaust is a myth devised by Jews to create support for the state of Israel. A fifth student denounces the fourth as anti-Semitic and demands an apology or appropriate punishment. What should you do?

This brief interchange raises enough issues to keep a class discussion going for weeks, under your capable direction, so you have no reason to be upset. Your students are off to a running start.

In the short run, though, there's the question of what to do now. The immediate issue before you is that one student wants another to apologize or be punished for what he said. Your response must be unequivocal: everyone in your class has a right to say what she or he thinks about the matter at hand. The fourth student may or may not choose to apologize but has no obligation to do so and will not be punished. And this stance, you should be clear, has nothing to do with your attitude toward the fourth student or the truth or falsity of what he said. As a general matter of academic freedom, no one will be punished for expressing an idea or viewpoint, no matter how offended or upset others may be (Principle 2).

That's the easy part. Now, what do you do next? One possibility is that you might attempt to direct further discussion by highlighting what seem to be two basic questions underlying the exchange: Did the Nazis commit genocide? If so, against what groups?

Where things go from here will depend on how students respond to your suggested questions and to each other. You cannot, and should not try to, determine what each student ends up believing, but you can and should share information and perspectives that you think at least some students in the class will find useful. As the discussion proceeds, for example, you may present the definition of genocide in the United Nations Genocide Convention and perhaps some alternative definitions. You may present facts about Nazi oppression of various groups relevant to determining whether various criteria for genocide are met.

You may point out how people reach different conclusions because they interpret evidence differently or apply different definitions. You may also point out that, despite this, there is often some consensus. In the present case, for example, you may note there is a scholarly consensus that (at the very least) the Nazis committed genocide, by any reasonable definition of that term, against Jews and Gypsies. You may also remind students, however, that even a scholarly consensus can be wrong. In the end, there is no substitute for getting the evidence you need, including evidence about what experts think and why, and making your best judgment about what to believe.

Suppose the fourth student continues to make what you deem to be disparaging and irrelevant comments about Israel. Ask yourself how long you would tolerate favorable comments about Israel. It is a fundamental violation of freedom of belief to restrict expression on the basis of viewpoint. Freedom of expression in academic contexts, however, is limited to matters "relevant to the curriculum" (Principle 2). You do have the authority to keep the focus of discussion on the Holocaust and may insist that discussion of Israel should be saved for after class. First, however, ask yourself (again) whether you really are acting on the basis of relevance, not viewpoint.

Now suppose the fifth student objects to the entire discussion, urging that academic freedom does not extend to Holocaust denial. Everyone knows the Nazis committed genocide against the Jews. To ask for evidence and urge discussion about this is to cast doubt on the truth.

You might reassure this student that you and other historians have no doubt about the reality of the Holocaust. The reality of the Holocaust can be doubted in your classroom only because everything can be doubted in your classroom. You might add that doubt and discussion often lead to deeper understandings and better-justified commitments.

Case 7–2 *As a history teacher in the United States, you have been directed to use a U.S. history textbook that highlights the role of U.S. forces in halting the Nazi extermination of the Jews, which it calls "the ultimate genocide in human history." Elsewhere, the text mentions briefly that Native Americans succumbed to alcohol and disease during the "European peopling of the Americas." You believe that the European conquest of the Americas in the centuries following 1492 was a genocidal process of far greater magnitude than the Holocaust and also of greater relevance to your American students. What should you do?*

In the long run, you should identify one or more books that are more accurate and comprehensive in their coverage of what you deem important to your students and should lobby for these books to be available for use as texts, or (even better) for the right to make your own text selections (Principle 4a). How you proceed will depend on the structure of governance in your school or college, whether there is an institutional tradition of academic freedom and faculty commitment to defending that freedom, and (in a public school or college) whether the existing selection process is so transparently politicized as to violate the First Amendment.

In the short run, however, let's assume you are stuck with this book. If education in your classroom is a direct transmission of information from textbook to student minds, then all is lost. Your students will learn false information from this text and will not learn anything else.

Presumably, however, this is not how you construe education in your classroom or any other. For students of all ages, learning history is an active process of constructing historical concepts, images, narratives, and explanations on the basis of information and ideas gleaned from multiple sources. The text is an important source, but you set the context within which it will be read and interpreted. At least to some extent, moreover, you are free to supplement it.

Just how much freedom you have depends in part on the state of academic freedom where you teach. Even an institution that restricts your autonomy in text selection may, and should, accord you substantial discretion to (a) provide analysis and critique with regard to claims and perspectives in the text and (b) supplement the text with additional information and ideas.

Thus, with regard to the role of the United States in halting the Holocaust, you can provide and discuss evidence that U.S. policy during World War II was not concerned with saving Jews. With regard to the description of the Holocaust as "the ultimate genocide in human history," you can reexamine the Holocaust in the context of other genocides and raise questions about whether and in what sense any of these can be considered "ultimate."

Regarding what the text blandly refers to as the "European peopling of the Americas," you can present an alternative picture of this centuries-long process as a succession of ethnic cleansings and geno-cides that killed millions of individuals and destroyed hundreds of culturally distinct groups. You can explain why you think these events, taken together, can be construed as a genocidal process of greater magnitude than the Holocaust. You need not and should not insist that the text is wrong and you are right. It should suffice to explain why you and many historians disagree with the perspective presented in the text. You can also provide examples from the history of your own region to highlight the special relevance of these matters for your students.

Even if you are free in principle to criticize and supplement the text as you please, you may be unable to fully meet what you see as your academic responsibilities. There may not be time left after explaining text material to add very much to it. There may be required exams that fail to assess what you think most important and thus penalize your students if you spend too much time on such matters. And you may have justifiable fears about how much protection your academic freedom will provide if students or parents challenge what you teach.

Nevertheless, you owe your students a curriculum devised on aca-demic rather than political grounds (Principle 4a). Whatever other obligations and concerns you may have, your professional responsibil-ity as a history teacher is to teach the truth about history, as best you can determine it, without regard to political or other pressures.

Case 7–3   *You are a student who grew up learning to be proud of your ancestors, who fought savage Indians to secure the land you live on. You are offended to be taught in school that they were guilty of genocide. You complain to the teacher, who responds that you grew up with one point of view and that an important part of education is exposure to alternative points of view. But if the school has to present the Indian point of view, you think, shouldn't it give at least equal time to the point of view of the settlers? Should you pursue your complaint?*

You have a right to explain and defend the perspective of your ancestors and other settlers and try to convince your classmates and the teacher that this perspective is at least as legitimate as that of the Indians (Principle 2). If the teacher forbids you to say what you think about this, or humiliates you for doing so, you should indeed pursue a complaint.

You do not have a right to determine the curriculum (Principle 4a), however, nor does academic freedom require a curriculum that accords equal time to every viewpoint (Principle 4b). Your teacher may have legitimate reasons for highlighting some viewpoints and providing less attention to others. Your teacher may have found, for example, that the settler point of view is well understood by nearly all students and that the indigenous viewpoint is not, thus suggesting the need for a curricular emphasis on the latter.

Rather than pursue a complaint demanding equal time, you should think about what is missing from the course, do your own research if necessary, and say whatever you think needs to be said. You should also listen carefully to alternative views, keeping in mind that even if the viewpoint you grew up with is not wrong, it may not be the whole story.

Case 7–4   *As a history teacher, you are preparing to show your students a historical movie that includes gruesome scenes of intense violence. You are concerned about student and parent reactions. What should you do?*

Your goal as a history teacher is to educate, not to shock, but much of history is shocking. Gruesome depictions of violence may generate emotional reactions that interfere with understanding, but they may also help students connect emotionally with historical events. There is no simple answer to the question of how much violence to show to students of various ages in various educational contexts.

With this in mind, you should be prepared to defend any movie you show, as you would defend any other portion of your curriculum. Be clear in your own mind about the reasons for showing this movie. If you believe the movie has sufficient educational value, either because of or in spite of the violence it depicts, you should arrange to show it. Be prepared to respond to concerns about the violence and to provide an alternative assignment in individual cases as appropriate. If you conclude that the educational value of the movie is marginal, see if you can find a better alternative.

One complicating factor is that your school may have rules requiring administrative or parental notification with regard to movies in general or specified categories of material, such as movies with restrictive age ratings due to violent or sexual content. Violating such rules could cost you your job, and you should certainly be aware of that. Following such rules, however, could cost you your professional self-respect if you believe you are compromising the education of your students out of self-interest. In some cases, changing the rules may be an option. In all cases, you should be aware of the relevant rules and risks, and make an informed decision about how to proceed.

Case 7–5 *You are an administrator who has been directed by your governing board to initiate a thorough review of the history curriculum. In particular, the board will expect a report identifying any curricular elements that may undermine national pride and recommending enhancements that will promote patriotism. What should you do?*

Remind the board that you are not a historian and that both you and the board must respect the right of students to a history curriculum formulated on the basis of academic considerations (Principle 4a). This does not mean the history curriculum cannot be reviewed, but it has important implications for who conducts the review and on what basis. Certainly the history curriculum should not be designed to undermine national pride, but neither should it be designed to promote mindless patriotism.

In fact, you might explain to the board that a curriculum transparently devised to promote patriotism may alienate students who perceive that they are being indoctrinated, whereas a curriculum that frankly discusses historical wrongs may help students better appreciate their country as one with the courage to face its past and to permit individuals to think for themselves. With these considerations in mind, you may try to convince the board that no review of the history curriculum is necessary.

In addressing this issue there is no need to dispute the board's concern with national pride and patriotism, but neither should you accept uncritically a narrow conception of history education as the inculcation of patriotic ideas and values. Help the board see how a school system that provides an academically justifiable history curriculum—and encourages students to discuss and reflect on what they are learning—will generate educated individuals with well-justified pride in their nation's accomplishments, realistic knowledge of its shortcomings, and a thoughtful commitment to a better future.

Case 7–6   *A parent contacts you, the principal, to complain that her daughter is struggling in a history class that teaches history backwards, starting with the present. What should you do?*

A very general principle of conflict resolution is to begin trying to resolve the conflict at the lowest possible level and then, if this fails, proceed from there. Your first question to the parent, then, should be to ask whether she has talked with the teacher. If she has talked with the teacher, you should ask how the teacher responded and why she was not satisfied with this response. If she has not talked with the teacher you should suggest she do so, making it clear that if she is not satisfied she should get back in touch with you. If she refuses to talk with the teacher, you should ask why and should further encourage such a discussion if you think this may be useful, but you should not insist on this first step if it appears it would be useless.

Assuming the matter is not resolved, the next step is for you to talk with the teacher. Find out how the class is actually organized, and why, and get whatever evidence is available about how well students are learning and whether they are meeting appropriate standards. You should also review whatever more general evidence may be available for or against this approach.

You may determine, for example, that the instructor is not really teaching history backwards in the sense of proceeding from the present in a reverse chronological order but rather is teaching in a yo-yo fashion that begins in the present, jumps back twenty years and then proceeds to the present, jumps back forty years and then moves forward again, and so forth. Clarifying this may not resolve your concerns but is an important step in addressing the situation.

What rationale might the teacher have for beginning in the present? One obvious one is that students live in the present. The teacher may indicate that, based on his or her experience, students just don't see the relevance of history when it is taught traditionally. By beginning with issues of current concern to current students, a backwards or yo-yo approach to history may be more motivating and thus generate better performance.

Is there evidence of better or worse performance? Obviously you will want to support the teacher's approach if evidence shows that it is invariably superior to the traditional approach for all teachers and all students in all circumstances. Correspondingly, you will not be supportive if evidence shows that the approach in question is invariably inferior to the traditional approach for all teachers and all students in all circumstances. What you will likely find, however, is that available evidence is sketchy and inconclusive. The reality is that the relative effectiveness of various educational methodologies may vary greatly depending on the teacher, students, and circumstances. All other things being equal, moreover, it is likely that teachers do better when they teach in ways they deem effective than when they are forced to use methods they deem inadequate. Thus, although you should certainly be open to evidence, you should not expect that evidence will solve the problem.

You may get closer to a solution, however, if you consider not just specific evidence but general theoretical considerations based on broader research. In the present case, for example, intuition may suggest that students learn history by internalizing a story that goes from the past to the present. This suggests that hearing the story in that order will be most productive. This intuition, however, is based on an outmoded, empiricist view of learning as a relatively direct and passive internalization of what one experiences. Decades of research in cognitive, developmental, and educational psychology shows that understanding comes about through active mental efforts to construct and reconstruct knowledge. Backwards teaching, and especially yo-yo teaching, may encourage precisely the kind of mental activity that promotes understanding.

Even taking theory and research into account, however, it may remain unclear whether the backwards or yo-yo approach is better or worse than the traditional approach in the present case. If in doubt, you should respect the professional judgment of the teacher. This does not mean ignoring the parent's concern about her daughter's performance but it may suggest you need to redirect the parent's attention from the issue of instructional method to her daughter's performance in other courses, study methods, and interests. In the absence of clear evidence of a general problem it may do more harm than good to address a specific concern like this with a general change in instructional method for all students in a class, especially if this is contrary to the professional judgment of the teacher.

It might be argued that, in the absence of clear evidence for the superiority of some alternative approach, you should insist on a traditional approach. The problem with this is that clear evidence for the general superiority of some instructional approach to some other is hard to come by in any event, and impossible if the new approach cannot even be tried. Thus a stance of this sort, although intended to protect students from questionable methods, reinforces the status quo—regardless of its effectiveness.

Another possible objection to backwards or yo-yo teaching may be that connecting history to the present makes it more controversial. That may be true, but it is not a legitimate reason for rejecting this approach. Relevance to meaningful and important current controversies may be precisely what helps students see the value of history.

Case 7–7 *Your state legislature has passed a bill requiring that history be taught as factual, not constructed, and that U.S. history be taught in such a way as to inculcate American values—including democracy, pluralism, and capitalism. As a history teacher, what should you do?*

Depending on where you live and teach, parts of this case are not hypothetical. In 2006, for example, Florida passed legislation mandating that "American history shall be viewed as factual, not as constructed."

Part of the problem here is a confusion between two meanings of *history*. Sometimes we use the word *history* to refer to what actually happened in the past (did George Washington really cut down that cherry tree or didn't he?), whereas other times we use the word to refer to a narrative about what happened in the past (as when we say a historian has just written a new history of the American Revolution). If historical narratives were generally expected to be full and exact renderings of the past this distinction would be unnecessary, but no history (in the second sense of a narrative about the past) can ever include all of the facts of history (in the first sense of what really happened). Historians have no choice but to choose what facts are most important, what interpretations of these facts are most convincing, and what narrative rendering best conveys what happened. History, in the second sense, is always and inevitably constructed.

To say history is constructed, however, is not to deny that it is factual. Historical narratives are not intended to be works of fiction. They are judged against strict criteria of truth that would be inappropriate for judging fiction. History in the second sense can be seen as a rational reconstruction of history in the first sense, constrained by considerations of truth in ways that fiction is not. Thus there is no problem with the legislature's insistence that history is (in some sense) factual, but there is a major problem in the assumption that this means it is not constructed.

One can also raise serious questions about "American values." Are these values held by all Americans? Are they values held only, or mostly, by Americans? Are there any such values? Do democracy and capitalism require each other? Could they be independent of each other? Might they even be inconsistent with each other? These are great questions for students to consider as they learn history, but it would constitute indoctrination for you or anyone else to structure the history curriculum in such a way as to lead students to particular conclusions mandated by the legislature. In fact, the result would be a constructed history of the worst sort.

So what should you do? In the long run, you might want to work with others in a collective effort to change the law. In the short run, you should try to find creative ways to teach in a manner that meets legal requirements without undermining the integrity of history and education (see Case 6–8 for an analogous situation in science education). If that can't be done, however, you must choose between your obligation to the law and your obligation to your students. Obviously it would be foolish to ignore the potential consequences of violating the law. But you may decide to take a risk, and perhaps pay a price, in order to protect the academic freedom of your students. And your students may appreciate it if you let them know exactly what you are doing and why. This may, in fact, teach them more about American values and the nature of history than your legislature ever imagined.

Case 7–8   *Black History Month is here again and as an African American student you are tired of hearing about Martin Luther King Jr. and Rosa Parks and depressed at the prospect of yet another round of lessons on the horrors of slavery and the victimization of black people ever since. It appears, however, that your white teacher is gearing up to go over it all yet again. What should you do?*

First of all, you should be aware that your concerns are very likely shared by at least some other students. Unless someone speaks up, however, your teacher may not have a clue about this. Quite the contrary, she may assume Black History Month is for the benefit of black students and that she is doing you a favor by talking about slavery.

One option is to talk with the teacher about the curriculum. This should be done carefully and respectfully. It is not your role to determine the curriculum for your classmates (Principle 4a). But you and your classmates are the ones being educated, and the quality of your education may be much improved if you take an active role in designing it. Your best bet is to convince the teacher that you are serious about your education and want to work with her in devising a curriculum that is both intellectually respectable and relevant to your interests and concerns.

What if you think the curriculum is racist? You might be correct, and you certainly have a right to say what you think. If your teacher thinks you are accusing her of racism, however, this may interfere with the possibility of working with her to improve the curriculum. If possible you should focus on how to improve the quality of education for everyone and avoid accusations that may alienate potential allies.

What about the focus on slavery and victimization? Questions can be raised about how much attention is devoted to these and other topics and about whether the curriculum is too depressing. Keep in mind, however, that the purpose of the history curriculum is not to make you or your classmates feel good. The purpose is to teach students about history. Like it or not, slavery and other forms of victimization are an important part of American history.

What about Martin Luther King Jr. and Rosa Parks? The problem, presumably, is not that they are mentioned but that so many others get so little attention. "In general, changes that expand the curriculum are more likely to be defensible than changes that contract or restrict it" (Principle 4b). You can certainly suggest you would like to hear more about other African Americans who have been agents of history and not just its victims. Even if the curriculum remains unchanged, you can do your own research and enlighten your classmates and teacher.

Addressing these issues may take a lot of effort, and you may consider it unfair that you have to work so hard at your education. Perhaps the school should indeed have done better, but your hard work is not in vain. On the contrary, taking responsibility for your own education may provide long-term benefits beyond the present class. The school controls what you get tested on, but no one can stop you from learning whatever you decide to learn.

Chapter 8
Tolerating the Intolerant: Bad Words and Worse

Introducing a 1965 performance of his hilarious song "National Brotherhood Week" at the hungry i in San Francisco, Tom Lehrer remarked, "I know there are people in the world who do not love their fellow human beings, and I *hate* people like that." The audience laughed, but underlying the joke was a genuine issue that became an increasingly serious source of controversy over the remaining decades of the twentieth century—especially in educational institutions, often under the heading "political correctness." Educators continue to confront this issue today, both within the curriculum and in the regulation of student behavior. Should we teach tolerance? Can we? What should a school do regarding students who don't wish to learn tolerance (at least not as we define it) or don't wish to practice it (at least not by our rules)? What if the intolerant individuals are teachers or administrators? What if it's not clear who's being intolerant of whom? Is the suppression of intolerance itself an act of intolerance?

Case 8–1   *A man from Mexico, living in the United States, is stopped by local police who mistakenly think he might be responsible for a crime they are investigating. He does not speak English, and they do not speak Spanish. He resists arrest and ends up dying in police custody, leading to much local publicity. A white female student in an ethnic studies class discussing the event says the Mexican had lived in the United States long enough that he should have learned English. An African American male student responds that her ideas are "ridiculous" and "bullshit." Over the course of further discussion he maintains that he shouldn't have to listen to such views and that people like her are what is wrong with America. You're the teacher.*

Your central concern here should be to keep the discussion productive. The immediate challenge in the present case is that the second student has not just disagreed with the first but has expressed himself in a manner that may discourage the first student, and others who share her view, from continuing to participate. On the other hand, given what the first student said and the immediacy of the topic, the intensity of the second student's reaction is readily understandable. You don't want to protect the first student (and others with similar views) by silencing the second (and others who share his outrage).

One possibility in this case is to let the discussion continue without intervening. If neither student demands action against the other, and neither seems intimidated into silence, it is not clear that there is any problem for you to solve. If the quality of discussion seems to suffer from the lack of civility, however, you might try to nudge it in a more civil direction (without threatening anyone). You could point out, for example, that the first student has done nothing more than express her viewpoint, which she has a right to do. You might note that others have a right to disagree with her and to indicate the strength of their disagreement, but that terms like *ridiculous* and *bullshit* are more likely to generate defensive reactions than thoughtful discussion. With regard to the suggestion that we shouldn't have to listen to views we find absurd or upsetting you might note that we do have some freedom to decide what to listen to but that in some contexts, such as a class discussion, exposure to such views is an unavoidable consequence of free expression—and not necessarily a bad thing. And of course we all have a right to say that some kinds of people are what is wrong with America but such thinking, you might argue, is not likely to lead to a better America.

Case 8–2 *The female student in Case 8–1 complains to you, as an administrator, that the male student was personally insulting to her. His response in class, she says, is precisely the sort that routinely silences women, and the teacher exacerbated the problem by failing to take it seriously. What should you do?*

Case 8–1 is in fact a real case that occurred at the University of Nebraska–Lincoln during a period when I was serving as chair of my academic department (educational psychology). The class was offered by a different department and taught by a female adjunct hired by that department. The male student, however, was a master's student in my own department and the female student came to me because she wanted to see him punished. I talked with both students, separately and together, and noted the value of civil discussion, but concluded that there was no basis for me to take any formal action. I wish I could say that the female student came to understand the value of free discussion and respected my decision, but in fact I think she regarded me as a sexist male defending another sexist male. She continued her efforts to find some university official to punish him, but was unsuccessful.

There was a further consideration, however. The male student was in a program in counseling and his ability to work with diverse individuals, including women, was an important and legitimate requirement for his degree. If the present case were part of a pattern of hostility toward women, that indeed would be a problem I should not ignore. If there were no such pattern, however, I wouldn't want to create a problem for him. Fortunately, his advisor was someone I knew well and whose judgment I trusted. I told her everything I knew, emphasizing that I had seen no basis for action and was not suggesting she needed to do anything either. She appreciated the information but assured me that she saw no evidence that it was part of some larger pattern, and he ended up graduating without further incident.

I should note that I had one important advantage over most administrators in dealing with this sensitive situation. I was a tenured professor doing a stint as department chair as a favor to my department, with no intent of continuing for more than a few years and no interest in moving to a higher administrative position. Thus I didn't need to worry about what higher administrators would think or about the effect of this on my career. Few administrators have this luxury.

Case 8–3   *In a discussion of human rights, a student argues that fundamental rights include the right not to be discriminated against because of your sexual orientation. Another student says this sort of absurd claim shows the problem with vague notions of human rights. A third student agrees with the second, noting how vagueness leads to overly broad conceptions of rights that protect immoral behavior and evil people. A fourth student adds that human rights can't protect everyone and everything. The first student replies that human rights are, by definition, rights that protect all people. "Yeah, people," murmurs a fifth student, "not faggots." You're the teacher.*

This is a case that would put any teacher to the test. Understandably, you may feel increasingly disappointed and frustrated by the successive comments of the second, third, and fourth students. Even if you recognize the right of these three students to express their views, you may be tempted to penalize the fifth student for using the term *faggot*. You should resist this temptation, I suggest, not only out of respect for the rights of your students but also because, from an educational point of view, there are better options.

Principles of academic freedom apply fully to students. Your students, no less than you, have "an ultimate right to believe . . . whatever they believe" (Principle 1) and "a right to express their views and to discuss them with others" (Principle 2). These principles can be justified on both moral and educational grounds (see Chapter 4). Morally, respect for persons entails respect for their intellectual autonomy, even if you justifiably believe them to be less developed or less educated than yourself. Educationally, moreover, there is substantial evidence that learning and development are fostered by contexts of intellectual freedom.

It might be argued that freedom of expression is not absolute and that this is one of those cases where common sense demands some limitation. It is indeed true that restrictions on the time, place, or manner of expression can sometimes be justified, but we should be wary of relying on "common sense" to guide us in this regard. Rather, we should make sure any such restrictions are carefully delineated and justified, and that they are neutral with regard to viewpoint.

In academic contexts, in particular, freedom of expression may justifiably be limited to matters "relevant to the curriculum" (Principle 2). A student who persistently talks about "faggots" in a calculus class, for example, might justifiably be required to stick to the topic of calculus and ultimately penalized for failing to do so. A student who persistently interrupts a calculus class to endorse gay rights, however, should be equally subject to sanction. Viewpoint neutrality is key here. Legitimate limitations on classroom speech, moreover, should not be abused by applying a stricter standard of relevance to objectionable views. The fifth student in the present case may be expressing a highly objectionable view of gays and lesbians, and may be expressing it in a rather inarticulate way (a point to which I shall return), but the student is indeed expressing a view relevant to the topic under discussion.

It might be argued that what distinguishes the fifth student from the second, third, and fourth is not viewpoint but rather the use of the epithet *faggot*. Perhaps we cannot punish students for opposing gay rights—but can't we punish students who use terms so offensive to others in the class that their manner of expression, as distinct from their point of view, is an act of harassment? Otherwise some students may be so offended as to be silenced, thus denying them an equal opportunity to exercise their own academic freedom.

There is something to be said for this argument (see Principle 5a), but we must also recall that academic freedom protects the expression of all viewpoints, "even if those views are deemed to be false, absurd, offensive, or otherwise objectionable" (Principle 2). Academic freedom does not protect harassment, provided harassment is strictly defined as a pattern of actions specifically directed against a particular individual with the intent of humiliating, intimidating, or otherwise harming that individual. If a student were to repeatedly call someone else in the class a faggot, despite clear indication that the other student found this objectionable, that would be a serious offense not protected by norms of academic freedom. Reasonable people might disagree on exactly where one draws the line between offensive speech and harassment, but it should be clear that the comment of the fifth student in the present case falls far short of that line.

What, then, should you do? One option is not to say anything at all. Peer interaction has a dynamic of its own that can be highly effective in promoting development and education. Pronouncements from a teacher or other authority may undermine this. If you hold your tongue for a moment, other students may criticize the use of the term *faggot* and, precisely because they are peers, have more impact than you could possibly have had.

There is no guarantee this will happen, however. There may be a stunned silence as students wait to see your reaction. If you do not react, some may take this as acquiescence. The discussion may move on to something else, closing off your opportunity to use the present situation for educational purposes. Your own academic freedom as the teacher to decide how to proceed is based on the assumption that you are in the best position to judge what will be most educational for your students.

One excellent option, I suggest, is to ask the fifth student to clarify and justify his or her view. More specifically, you might, with seeming innocence, ask what is meant by *faggot* and why individuals in this category do not qualify as people. This response is, to be sure, a bit disingenuous. You are not directly accusing the student of making a snide and ignorant remark that fails to advance the discussion but you have no objection if the student or others make this inference. The student may be unpleasantly surprised to be asked to justify a comment that was not meant to be taken seriously, at least not in any academic sense. If the student has no meaningful response to your query, others in the class may conclude that comments of this sort are unjustifiable and some may go on to question the earlier facile rejections of gay rights. They may also come to see that intellectual discussions are more than just serial statements of diverse opinions. They may see that in your classroom they are free to say whatever they wish but that they should be prepared to explain and justify whatever they say.

It is possible, of course, that the student will indeed have some response. You can then proceed from there to state your own views about the use of terms like *faggot* or about the nature and scope of fundamental human rights.

Respect for a student's right to hold a particular opinion does not entail agreement with, or even respect for, that opinion. On the contrary, respect for students is fully consistent with the presentation of alternative views and with efforts to convince students to change their opinions. The key is that such efforts must not be, and must not be perceived to be, coercive. It should be clear both to you and your students that, in the end, they "have an ultimate right to believe and value whatever they believe and value, to maintain or change their beliefs and values as they choose, and to define themselves in terms of whatever beliefs and values they deem central to their identities" (Principle 1).

Case 8–4   *A class is discussing the psychological impact of discrimination on various groups. A student says that the major problem for gays is the psychological impact of Christian biases and bigotry. Another student says these remarks overlook the objective sinfulness of homosexuality and offend him as a Christian. Other students agree with the first that Christians are indeed, for the most part, homophobic bigots whose hateful rhetoric causes ongoing violence against gays and lesbians. The Christian student gets up to leave. What should you do as the teacher?*

Before getting to issues of academic freedom there is a question of whether, under school policy, the student is free to leave. Keep in mind that he may be angry and upset about what he perceives as a personal attack and an assault on his religion. He may have learned from past experience that it is important for him to get away and cool down when he feels too angry to maintain his composure. You may have an obligation to remind him of school rules, and perhaps to enforce them, but if at all possible you should not forbid him to leave.

Even if the student has a right to leave, however, you should try to convince him to stay, even if you believe that he is indeed a homophobic bigot and that his departure would help the class achieve a consensus consistent with your own views. There are at least three reasons for this. First, the departure of any student will obviously limit the education of that student. Your obligations to your students are not limited to those students who share your beliefs (Principle 5a). Second, if your specific intent is to educate students about sexual orientation and alleviate homophobia, homophobic students are precisely the audience you most need to reach. The departure of a possibly homophobic student, and the consequent alienation of other Christian or homophobic students, thus undermines the achievement of your pedagogical goals. Finally, given that the Christian student appears to represent a minority view in this class, his departure will decrease the diversity of views in your classroom. If other students perceive it as dangerous to share what they see as a disfavored view, moreover, the opportunity for productive discussion is greatly compromised.

What will it take to convince the Christian student to stay? Quite possibly, he might like to see you show your support for him personally (or for civil discussion in your classroom) by punishing those who have called him a homophobic bigot.

On a continuum from offensiveness to harassment, the present circumstances arguably fall a bit closer to harassment than those of Case 8–3. As offensive as the term *faggot* may be, no particular person was called a faggot in that case, whereas the Christian student in the present case heard Christians denounced as homophobic bigots immediately after he identified himself as a Christian who considers homosexuality sinful. He might believe the statements he found so offensive were aimed at him in particular with the intent to humiliate and silence him.

You have no reason to doubt, however, that the students who said most Christians are homophobic bigots genuinely believe this, and you must be clear with all your students that they have a right to hold and express this view. Even if students were to say that all Christians are homophobic bigots, an assertion that is demonstrably false, you must be clear that students have a right to believe this and a right to say what they believe. If some of your students follow the Christian student out of class and continue to berate him for his views after he has made it clear that he no longer wishes to discuss the issue, they may be crossing the line into harassment. Wherever that line may be, however, it clearly is not reached in the present case.

Unless the present case is part of a larger picture of targeted abuse, then there is no question of harassment. Without singling anyone out for punishment, however, there is much you can do to simultaneously support the offended student, support the students who have offended him, and turn the present situation to educational advantage. For a start, you can assure the Christian student as he heads for the door that you understand why he is upset, that you intend to seriously address what has just happened in the class, and that you believe his presence will enhance the discussion to follow. If possible, you should not *tell* him to stay but rather should *ask* him to stay, making it clear that you are requesting this not just because he has a right to be in the class but because you believe his potential contributions will enhance the educational value of the class.

How you proceed from this point will depend not only on whether the Christian student stays but also on what you know of the class and on how your students react to the situation. At the very least, you have an opportunity to encourage your students to avoid stereotyping, to express themselves in a civil manner, and to respect and value ideological diversity. You can and should promote these dispositions and values without censorship or punishment. In the short run, the most efficient way to ensure civil discussions in which no one is offended may be to set strict rules students must follow to avoid penalties. The resulting discussions, however, are likely to be not only civil but bland. In the long run, you want students to engage in civil and productive discussions out of respect for each other, not because you are watching.

What if the offended student is out the door before you have time to decide what to do and gone before you can go after him? You should not berate yourself for failing to devise Solomonic responses to difficult circumstances in the blink of an eye. The above considerations can direct you in discussing what just happened with the remaining students in the class. You can let them know that you hope to restore relations with the offended student, explain why, and invite them to assist you. Following through with the offended student may not only be the right thing to do for his sake but may also provide the rest of the class with a useful model of maintaining dialogue and community in the face of deep disagreements.

Case 8–5 *You are an administrator who receives a complaint from the student in Case 7–3. She says that her history teacher persists in denigrating her heritage by teaching that her pioneer ancestors were perpetrators of genocide. She no longer wants to attend that class. In fact, she'd like to see the teacher fired. What should you do?*

Obviously you need to know what is going on in this class before taking any action against the teacher. You might start by getting as much information as you can from the student. You should be clear with her that she has a right not to be unfairly and personally targeted but she doesn't have a right to hear only good things about people with whom she identifies (and the same would hold regardless of her ethnic background or ancestry). The history curriculum should be designed by historians and true to history (Principle 4a) and should be modified only if there are academic reasons for doing so (Principle 4b). If the student still believes she has been mistreated after you have clarified these principles, you will have a better idea about the nature of the potential problem and can then talk with the teacher to get more information.

Unless there has been deliberate harassment of a particular student, cases like this are best handled by focusing on the quality of education, not on wrongdoing by the teacher. Good teaching involves drawing students in, not antagonizing them. Perhaps there are ways of encouraging this teacher, and others, to reach out to students upset by what is taught. Perhaps there are ways of encouraging students to enhance the curriculum by providing their own ideas and, more generally, to take a more active role in their education (see Case 7–8). By maintaining a positive focus you may be able to redirect everyone's attention to improving education for everyone rather than succumbing to the needless assumption that a wrongdoer must be identified and punished.

Case 8–6 *You have been involved in the process of interviewing candidates for several teaching positions in your school. Among the candidates who appear highly qualified with regard to academic expertise and teach-*

ing ability are three whose interviews raised troubling considerations. One believes that students of African descent are, on average, less intellectually capable than those of other races. The second believes that homosexuality is a sin. The third believes that speech offensive to members of various minority groups must be restricted in order to maintain a positive educational environment for those individuals. Should these beliefs be considered in making your hiring decisions?

However objectionable you find some or all of these beliefs, they should not in themselves be a basis for hiring decisions (Principle 1). Your obligation to hire the best teacher, however, does require attention to some related issues. The person you hire should be able and willing to teach all students regardless of their ancestry, sexual orientation, or political views. People have a right to believe whatever they believe but employees also have an obligation to do their jobs, and you have an obligation to evaluate applicants' ability and motivation to do what the advertised jobs require. You should not make inferences from beliefs alone but you should seek and attend to evidence about the quality of teaching. Whatever someone believes about African ancestry or homosexuality in general, as a teacher that person has a responsibility to teach and evaluate individual students fairly. Whatever a teacher believes about offensive speech, she or he has a responsibility to respect the First Amendment rights and intellectual freedoms of students. Your responsibility is to hire teachers who will do their jobs well.

Some beliefs may make it more difficult for some people to do certain jobs but you should not presume inability to teach based on beliefs alone. Teachers who question the capability or morality of various categories of people may be fully dedicated to teaching all students. Teachers horrified by what they see as hate speech may recognize their obligations to the First Amendment. Each applicant should receive full and fair consideration.

Difficult cases may be minimized by communicating job expectations early and forthrightly. Schools should be clear that they aim to promote the learning and development of all students and that this includes respect for their intellectual freedom. Potential teachers should be encouraged to reflect on whether teaching—in general, or in particular settings—is consistent with their personal and professional beliefs, values, and goals.

Chapter 9

The Birds, the Bees, and the Censors: Sex Education and Its Discontents

When the birds flock, they chirp, they sing, they peck, and they soar. As for the bees, they buzz, sting, and attend to their queen. But when the birds and the bees get together, it's all about sex.

Well, not really. Actually it's all about sex education, which is only partly about sex.

In any event, whatever birds and bees do, they don't do it with each other—and they certainly don't write about it or discuss its intricacies. Human beings, on the other hand, have plenty to say about sex—and strong notions about what should (or should not) be said to children, what should (or should not) be said in various circumstances, and what should never be said at all.

Sexuality, in fact, is routinely deemed a topic so extraordinary as to require and justify special forms of censorship. In the adult world, this can be seen in the constitutional concept of obscenity as a category of expression outside the bounds of the First Amendment. But sexual speech that falls far short of obscenity—which has a relatively narrow and technical legal definition—may be deemed objectionable in educational contexts, especially with regard to children. Those empowered to control sexual discourse in academic contexts often assume that sexuality is not subject to standard principles of academic freedom. In addition to overt censorship, moreover, teachers and students routinely limit or avoid sexual topics and ideas because of their highly controversial nature. But there are always those who push back.

"A censor pronouncing a ban," wrote the Nobel Prize–winning novelist and critic J. M. Coetzee, "is like a man trying to stop his penis from standing up." Recalling Saint Augustine's observation that the sexual organs "move independently of the will," Coetzee noted that "not even the guardians of our morals" are exempt from "this disobedience of the flesh." The "spectacle" of censorial efforts to control the "unruly member" struck him as simply "ridiculous." Even with regard to children, Coetzee suggested, censorship may be more dangerous and harmful than sexuality. But censorship is apparently as human and universal as sexuality itself, and nowhere is this more apparent than in educational contexts. And so, in this chapter, we turn to the birds, the bees, and the censors—an academic ménage à trois.

Case 9–1 *You are about to begin teaching a unit on sexuality. A student in your class finds the planned content offensive and pornographic and does not wish to participate in this portion of the course. What should you do?*

Your response to this situation should be based on general considerations concerning course requirements and student rights rather than on anything specific to the topic of sexuality. Students may have profound objections to many things that go on in many courses. They may not want to read an assigned novel, may not want to learn about scientific topics such as evolution or global warming, or may not want to hear about disturbing historical events. In general, educational institutions may legitimately require that students meet certain requirements to pass a course, graduate, or receive a particular degree. To whatever extent possible, however, they should try to accommodate individual students, especially where students have sincere objections based on deeply held beliefs. Thus an English teacher may assign an alternative novel to a student who objects to the assigned novel. In most cases the original novel, although appropriate and valuable, is not the only one that could have been assigned and is not a necessary condition for certifying that the student has met an appropriate standard for passing the course. On the other hand, a biology teacher may decide that an understanding of evolution is so basic to a particular biology course, and so infused throughout the text and curriculum, that no alternative can take its place.

With these considerations in mind, you should decide how central the present unit on sexuality is to the course you are teaching and whether there are alternatives that would maintain the integrity of the course and its requirements. You should accommodate the student if at all possible, but you should not give any student a grade that misrepresents the student's competence or achievement.

What if the student tells you what changes in the unit will make it acceptable? If it appears that minor adjustments will make the sexuality unit more acceptable to this student and perhaps others without compromising your educational goals, you should thank the student and make the changes. If the changes are not ideal but seem tolerable, you should not compromise the education of other students but should see if you can accommodate this particular student. If the changes will undermine the academic integrity or legitimate educational goals of the course, however, you should not make adjustments simply to pacify the student.

What if you decide not to make any accommodation and the student then complains to an administrator who warns you that the school faces an upcoming decision vital to its funding for the next several years and that this is not the time to be stirring up controversy? Obviously you should not be stirring up needless controversy, especially at an inopportune time, and you may look harder for a solution acceptable to everyone. If no such solution can be found, however, your central obligation is to the academic integrity of the curriculum and the associated requirements—not to keeping students, administrators, or the general public happy.

What if the student continues to emphasize the pornographic nature of what you are teaching? Presumably you don't want to be known as a purveyor of pornography and this language may tempt you either to back down, which is probably the intent, or else to deny that you are teaching pornography. It is important to keep in mind, however, that *pornography* is a term with no clear meaning and, in itself, no legal status. Thus there is no point in arguing about whether some aspect of your course is *really* pornographic. Pornography is very much in the eye of the beholder. The student is entitled to express his or her feelings by using this term but you should keep your focus on the nature and educational value of what is being taught.

Case 9–2   *A couple does not want their daughter exposed to a secondary school sex education curriculum but the daughter wants to learn what is taught in this portion of her health class and insists to the teacher and principal that she be permitted to continue in the class. The teacher and principal ask you, as associate superintendent for curriculum, for guidance.*

This case is greatly complicated by the disagreement between the parents and their daughter. Such a case is unlikely at the elementary school level, where parental decisions are typically taken as family decisions and children are unlikely to press an independent point of view. Such a case is also unlikely in higher education, where most students have reached the age of majority. In secondary education, however, most students are still minors subject to parental authority. This is a legal fact you cannot ignore, but you should not proceed on the assumption that adolescents are simply large children. Extensive research on adolescent reasoning and rationality shows that adolescents have competencies far beyond those of children and comparable to those of adults. The daughter may in fact be mature enough to have made a reasonable judgment about what she wants and needs to learn, and there may be good reason to support that judgment. Nevertheless, you cannot ignore the parents, nor do you wish to set a precedent that you may come to regret. You should probably check with an attorney about your legal options and then formulate a general policy to cover cases of this sort. Such a policy must of course recognize the legal rights of parents, but it should also recognize that children are not the property of their parents and that adolescent development is in large part the development of personal autonomy. As an educator, your central concern should be to maximize educational opportunity for all students.

Case 9–3   *A student in your class is researching student First Amendment rights and you recommend Nat Hentoff's* The First Freedom: The Tumultuous History of Free Speech in America, *which is available in the school library. She takes the book home and before long her father calls to complain that he was shocked to find an "obscene" poem in a book you recommended to his daughter. The poem, written by fifteen-year-old Jody Caravaglia, is entitled "The City to a Young Girl." It begins:*

> *The city is*
> *One million horny lip-smacking men*
> *Screaming for my body.*
> *The streets are long conveyor belts*
> *Loaded with these suckling pigs.*
> *All begging for*
> *a lay*

a little pussy
a bit of tit
a leg to rub against
a handful of ass
the connoisseurs of cunt

The poem goes on to describe how, day and night, they press in on her "closer and closer." "I swat them off like flies," she writes, "but they keep coming back" because, she concludes, "I'm a good piece of meat." The father doesn't want his daughter reading such things. What should you say?

Consider first the charge of obscenity. You need not and should not reject the father's distaste for the poem, and can acknowledge his use of the term "obscene" as a reflection of how offensive he found it, but the poem is not legally obscene. Without delving into the morass of obscenity law, you could note that the poem is not intended to get the reader sexually aroused. Quite the contrary.

Your primary focus, however, should not be on the poem itself but the larger context. You recommended this book because it was relevant to the student's project. The poem is in the book because it was at the center of a major First Amendment controversy. The poem was a center of controversy because the present father is not the first to find it objectionable, and you can point this out in a way that to some extent validates his concerns. But at the same time you can note that the poem originally appeared in an anthology entitled *Male & Female Under 18* that was in a school library in Chelsea, Massachusetts, and that remained in the library (despite being challenged) because the effort to remove it was deemed by a federal judge to be a violation of the First Amendment—which is precisely what your student is researching. You should urge the father to support his daughter's education by letting her know what he thinks but leaving it to her to decide whether and how to pursue this project.

If the father remains adamant that he must protect his daughter from this poem you should of course acknowledge that she is indeed *his* daughter, not yours, and that it is not your role to control her upbringing. If she subsequently returns the book and wishes to modify her project you should respect her decision, even if you suspect the decision is not entirely hers. On the other hand, if she wishes to continue the project over her father's objections, your situation becomes much more complicated and you should probably seek guidance from an appropriate administrator regarding school policy, which may turn out to be unclear (see Case 9–2).

Finally, there is the possibility that the father will not be satisfied to control his own daughter's reading but will insist that the book be removed from the school library or that you refrain from recommending books like this to any students. To accede to such demands, you must insist, would infringe on the rights of other students and other parents (not all of whom wish to restrict their children in the same ways). You should try to convince the present father that he has no legitimate authority beyond his own daughter and that whatever further action he chooses to take is most likely to succeed if he limits his demands with this in mind. If he nevertheless proceeds in an effort to remove the book from the library or to restrict faculty from recommending books that go beyond the general curriculum, you should of course oppose this as inconsistent with the intellectual freedom of students and the proper role of teachers and librarians.

Case 9–4   *As part of a school assembly associated with a forthcoming student government election, student Matthew Fraser has just given the following speech on behalf of one of the candidates:*

> *I know a man who is firm—he's firm in his pants, he's firm in his shirt, his character is firm—but most of all, his belief in you, the students of Bethel, is firm.*
>
> *Jeff Kuhlman is a man who takes his point and pounds it in. If necessary, he'll take an issue and nail it to the wall. He doesn't attack things in spurts—he drives hard, pushing and pushing until finally— he succeeds.*
>
> *Jeff is a man who will go to the very end—even the climax, for each and every one of you.*
>
> *So vote for Jeff for A.S.B. vice–president—he'll never come between you and the best our high school can be.*

Students find the speech hilarious but, as principal, you are worried that some might have been offended and that some parents might hear about the speech and complain. What should you do?

This is an actual case that began in 1983 at Bethel High School in Pierce County, Washington, with the above speech. Kuhlman won the election by a large margin, but the one-minute endorsement resulted in Fraser being suspended for two days and denied the opportunity to speak at graduation. Fraser sued, arguing on the basis of *Tinker v. Des Moines* (1969) that, in the absence of any disruption, the school had no authority to censor his speech or punish him for it. A federal judge ruled in his favor and this decision was upheld by the Ninth Circuit Court of Appeals, which would normally have been the end of the case. But the school convinced the U.S. Supreme Court to hear its appeal, and in *Bethel v. Fraser* (1986) the court reversed the earlier judgment, ruling that Fraser was a "confused boy" whose speech was "plainly offensive to both teachers and students." Justice John Paul Stevens, dissenting, questioned how what was offensive to students could be determined by "a group of judges who are at least two generations and 3,000 miles away from the scene of the crime." But the majority opinion by Chief Justice Warren Burger, without overruling *Tinker*, proceeded to carve out an unprecedented exception to the First Amendment for speech deemed by a school to be inconsistent with "the habits and manners of civility."

Analyzing the decision, *New York Times* education reporter Fred Hechinger took particular note of the majority's concern that Fraser's speech was, as Chief Justice Burger put it, "acutely insulting to teenage girl students."

> The Chief Justice may have been motivated by old-fashioned chivalry; but in the contemporary context, [his opinion] has a sexist ring. Should high-school girls be sent out of the room when Shakespeare's "lewd" ways of dealing with male sexuality and his frequent sexual metaphors and innuendo appear in literature classes? (Hechinger 1986, 20)

Hechinger was right that from the perspective of the 1980s the notion that girls and women need special protection from sexual expression had come to be seen by many as a sexist relic of the past. But the chief justice may have had the last laugh here. Over the next few years, with the rise of concern about sexual harassment, the notion that girls and women need special protection from sexual expression returned with a vengeance, and by the early 1990s became a major rationale for singling out sexuality as a special topic outside the usual norms of intellectual and academic freedom (see Case 9–8).

In light of the court's *Hazelwood* decision less than two years later (see Chapter 3), *Bethel v. Fraser* can now be seen as the beginning of the end for First Amendment protection of students' intellectual freedom. There is nothing in either decision, however, that requires censorship. Schools remain free to respect the intellectual freedoms of their students. In the present case there was no evidence that anyone was offended by Fraser's speech other than school officials and members of the court. Even if someone in the audience had been offended, moreover, there was no principled basis for deeming offensiveness an exception to the First Amendment, nor could such an exception be justified by the sexual content of the speech. Under the present principles, Bethel High School had no justification for punishing Matthew Fraser, and (despite the precedent set by this decision) schools continue to have good reason to respect the intellectual freedoms of their students—even when they choose to talk about sex.

Case 9–5   *As a school librarian you are directed to remove several books concerning sexual orientation from the school library and to seek special approval before purchasing any other books related to this topic. What should you do?*

As children's books addressing sexual orientation and related matters have become increasingly common since the 1980s, censorship of such books has become one of the major categories of censorship in the United States. Your obligation as a school librarian is to select books on the basis of academic criteria and to resist efforts to remove books from the library unless there is good reason to believe their selection was unjustified (see Principle 4b). You should make sure your school system has a policy in place regarding the selection and removal of library books and that it follows this policy consistently. If the policy is deemed inadequate it should perhaps be revised—but under no circumstances should you accede to special rules or exceptions for matters of sexuality or any other particular topic.

Many books challenged in relation to sexual orientation—especially books such as *Daddy's Roommate* and *Heather Has Two Mommies* that are aimed at children and purchased by elementary schools—focus on same-sex relationships and related family matters (usually involving children) rather than on sexuality per se. This is something you might point out to parents or others concerned about the age-appropriateness of books in an elementary school library. School librarians do consider the age of students in selecting books for a school library, and rightly so. It is important, however, not to press this point too far. Any general rule forbidding reference to sexuality in elementary schools or in books about same-sex relationships would be contrary to the present principles of academic freedom, which make no exception for sexuality.

Case 9–6   *The school newspaper for which you serve as advisor (and teacher of the associated journalism class) is planning to run articles about safe sex and condom distribution in schools. You know the articles will be controversial and think they may not be fully accurate. What should you do?*

There are two quite different issues here. It is part of the role of a newspaper to inform readers about controversial issues, but the newspaper will fail to be informative if its articles are inaccurate. As the advisor it is your role to encourage good journalism, and this may justify refusing to publish bad journalism—but it is not your role to censor controversial content.

To take an analogy, suppose you were a health teacher receiving one of these articles as a paper in your class. It would violate the academic freedom of your student if you were to give the paper a low grade because it addresses a controversial topic or expresses controversial views. But it would not violate any principle of academic freedom for you to give the paper a low grade because it falls short of legitimate standards of accuracy. As the advisor to a school newspaper intended to help educate students in journalism, your evaluation of the quality of student work leads not just to grades but also to decisions about whether the work merits publication in the newspaper. Refusing to publish an article is like giving a paper a low grade. This is not necessarily censorship but it could be depending on your reason. Your role as the newspaper advisor requires that your judgments be made entirely on journalistic grounds.

Your principal, it should be noted, may have other motivations and under *Hazelwood* may have the legal authority to reverse your judgment about this. Academically, however, for the principal to censor an article you think worthy of publication is no different than for the principal to lower a grade you have given to a student project. You are the journalism expert, not the principal. In the context of a particular controversy, it may be impossible to convince the principal to respect your judgment, but at a quieter time you should advocate school policies that protect your academic freedom and that of your students, not because such a policy is legally required (it probably isn't) but because it is educationally advantageous.

Case 9–7 A teacher endorses masturbation as preferable to sexual relationships for young teens. As the responsible administrator you are receiving complaints. How should you respond?

Assuming the complaint is at least minimally credible, you should investigate the facts. Suppose, for example, the teacher is a math teacher who spent most of a class period discussing teen sex. In this case, there is no need to delve into exactly what the teacher said. Academic freedom is limited to matters "relevant to the curriculum" (Principle 2). Students take this class to learn math, not to hear whatever views the teacher may wish to express on whatever topics happen to interest him or her. If this is an isolated incident, a reminder about the boundaries of academic freedom may be sufficient. If it is part of a larger pattern, however, the instructor is taking advantage of a captive audience of students, and you may have to take stronger action.

Suppose, instead, the teacher is responsible for teaching about sexuality and urges young teens to avoid sexual relationships. In response to a student question about sexual outlets, the teacher suggests that masturbation is preferable to sexual relationships at this age. You might or might not have answered the question the same way, but you are not the teacher and have no reason to take action. President Clinton fired Surgeon General Jocelyn Elders in 1994 for a statement like this, but that was a matter of politics. As an educational administrator your commitment must be to education, and education is best served by respecting the expertise and autonomy of your teachers.

Suppose, finally, the comment was made outside of class in response to a student question or was published in the local newspaper. Here the guiding principle is that a teacher, like anyone else, has a right to express his or her beliefs (Principle 2). There is no exception for matters of sexuality.

Case 9–8 A female teacher in a human sexuality class uses a banana to illustrate the application of a condom, joking that one should always be prompt because men, like basketball players, sometimes dribble before they shoot. A male student complains to several administrators that her objectification of the penis created a hostile academic environment for him as a man. What should be done?

This is a real case from the University of Nebraska–Lincoln in which I was involved as an informal advisor to the teacher. The student, she said, was upset with her because (among other things) she had objected to his coming to class drunk. His claim that she had created a "hostile academic environment" for him "as a man," she maintained, showed only that he had carefully studied the language of sexual harassment regulations in his effort to make trouble for her. Although she was never found guilty of sexual harassment, she spent much of the next year justifying her teaching to administrators and waiting to see what would happen, and eventually left Nebraska in disgust. Others responsible for teaching about sexuality watched this case with concern, and some for whom sexuality was an optional topic chose to stop teaching about it.

Educational institutions are, of course, right to ban harassment. The problem is that policies concerning harassment are often so vague, and so focused on sexuality, that a teacher or student wishing to avoid a charge of harassment must avoid saying anything that might offend anyone—especially with regard to sexuality. Individuals, as the principles of academic freedom make clear, have a right to believe whatever they choose about matters of sexuality and to express their views even if those views are deemed offensive or otherwise objectionable. Broad and vaguely worded sexual harassment policies effectively create a right not to be offended with regard to sexual matters. It is inconsistent with academic freedom, however, to limit freedom of expression to the expression of ideas that will not be deemed offensive. There is no reason to think sexuality requires a special exception to the right to hold and express ideas that offend others.

Harassment, strictly defined, is a pattern of actions specifically directed against a particular individual with the intent of humiliating, intimidating, or otherwise harming that individual. Thus defined, harassment is not protected by norms of academic freedom regardless of the sexual content of any ideas that may be expressed as part of the act of harassment. Sexual harassment is wrong because it is harassment, not because it is sexual. Unfortunately, in the broader context of concern about sexuality, education, and children, sexual harassment policies often serve to keep sexuality out of the curriculum and remain a major threat to academic freedom.

Case 9–9   *The state legislature is considering a bill requiring that education about sexuality highlight the importance of abstaining from sexual intercourse until marriage and that it not include any consideration of means for preventing pregnancy or disease except for evidence that such means are unreliable. Members of the legislature propose three amendments. One would limit the educational requirements set by the bill to cover only public educational institutions. A second would exempt colleges and universities. A third would delete the restriction on education about preventing pregnancy and disease, leaving only a requirement to highlight the virtues of abstinence. As a state legislator, how will you vote on each amendment and on the bill as a whole? What if you were a member of an educational governing board considering an abstinence-only proposal?*

The central problem with this bill is that curriculum should not be determined by the state legislature (Principle 4a). Each of the amendments would make the bill less objectionable but, even if they all pass, this central problem would remain. The first of the three amendments recognizes that the legislature has limited authority over private education but fails to recognize the proper limits on its authority over public education. The second recognizes the danger of legislative control over college education but fails to recognize the need for academic freedom in elementary and secondary education as well.

The final amendment recognizes that contracting the curriculum is, in general, a more serious problem than expanding it (Principle 4b). Abstinence from sex does indeed have major advantages and most sexuality educators already teach this, so an amended bill that does not forbid teaching about ways of preventing pregnancy and disease would not require any change in the curriculum. Thus the three amendments probably make this a bill everyone can live with, but it is still wrong in principle and a dangerous precedent for future legislative meddling.

Educational governing boards are closer to education than state legislatures and legitimately make education-related decisions that would constitute micromanagement if made by a legislature. School board members are no more likely than state senators, however, to be experts on, say, physics, history, literature, or sexuality. Curriculum decisions should be left to teachers and experts with relevant expertise (Principle 4a). This is not to say that experts always make the best decisions. But experts on sexuality are more likely than governing board members or state legislators to make curriculum decisions about sexuality on the basis of relevant research rather than political ideology, religious commitment, or popular opinion.

Chapter 10

Doing Right and Being Good: Morality, Values, and Character

S hould education address issues of morality, values, and/or character? The careful wording of this question reflects the difficulty
of answering it. Morality, values, and character are related concepts but they are not identical. Moral education, values education,
and character education overlap substantially but also differ in
important ways. Subtle distinctions in terminology may mask fundamental differences in goals and methods. Even if we agree that education should "address" one or more of these, what exactly should
teachers do? Provide some kind of experience? Teach particular ideas?
Model or require good behaviors? Forbid bad behaviors? Instill per-
sonality traits? Promote development?

Education always involves knowledge and skills. Issues of academic freedom often arise when our concern with knowledge goes
beyond unquestioned facts to matters of interpretation and perspective, or when our concern with skills goes beyond reading and writing to analysis and critical thinking. In this chapter, however, we go
even further, connecting education to matters of doing what is right
and being a good person. In this realm the potential for, and danger
of, indoctrination may be particularly great. Should public schools
avoid addressing matters of morality, values, and character? Should
such matters be left to families and to private schools chosen by parents with shared values? Can principles of academic freedom help us
distinguish education from indoctrination with regard to morality,
values, and character?

Case 10–1 *You are a teacher at a school that has decided to promote
character by approving and promoting an official list of core virtues: justice, compassion, tolerance, respect, honesty, diligence, courage, loyalty,*

and responsibility. It is expected that every teacher will play a role in the school's effort by regularly extolling these virtues. What should you do?

Character education programs vary greatly but most are centered on a set of core virtues such as those listed here. At first glance, such lists always seem reasonable, even admirable. If the graduates of your school turn out to be just, compassionate, tolerant, respectful, honest, diligent, courageous, loyal, and responsible, who could possibly object? But there is much more to be said about exactly what the school is trying to accomplish, about the means it is using, and about what you should do. For a start, it is worth looking more closely at the specific virtues.

Justice and compassion, the first two virtues listed, are specifically *moral* virtues in that they involve the rights and welfare of others. Justice involves our obligation to fair treatment of all people, including matters of equality and due process. Compassion involves caring enough about others to help them in ways that go beyond the minimal obligations of justice. But how do we know what is just? Who should we help, and when? Can compassion for specific others interfere with the promotion of justice for all? Already there are complications.

Tolerance, respect, and honesty might also seem, at first, to be moral virtues. But tolerance for injustice may be immoral. And many schools have zero-tolerance policies with respect to drugs, weapons, violence, or whatever else they deem intolerable. They may even, paradoxically, have zero tolerance for intolerance (see Chapter 8). Zero-tolerance policies may be misguided but they remind us that tolerance for everything is not necessarily a virtue. There are serious questions about what we should tolerate and when. Similarly, respect for authority may lead to believing what you are told to believe and doing what you are told to do, regardless of whether it is moral. Who exactly should we respect, and what exactly does this entail? As for honesty, it may sometimes be moral to withhold information, or even lie, in order to protect someone from harm. Obviously we don't want our students to be intolerant, disrespectful, and dishonest, but it is not so clear exactly what we do want.

As for diligence, courage, loyalty, and responsibility, it seems likely that the September 11 hijackers rated high in all of these areas. These and other personal and social virtues help individuals and groups achieve their goals regardless of the morality of those goals. These are nonmoral virtues that can serve a variety of purposes.

What, then, should you do? You can certainly advocate any or all of these virtues without compromising your students' academic freedom, but such advocacy may have little or no effect. Stronger exhortations may be indoctrinative and, given the likelihood of student resistance, counterproductive. Instead, you might point out to students that all of these "virtues" are important concepts worth thinking about and discussing. A brief critique of the virtues along the lines noted above, and some compelling examples, might do more to generate reflection and discussion than simply exhorting students to be virtuous in these various ways. This may not be what the school had in mind but it addresses questions of character without indoctrinating your students. If your commitment to character education is questioned, you can note that you are indeed educating students about character, and that the school should respect your academic freedom so you can fulfill your academic responsibilities. This might even teach the school a thing or two about respect and responsibility.

Case 10–2 *As a teacher committed to academic freedom you don't want to force your own values on your students, but you also don't want to neglect the realm of values. Your solution is to present your students with dilemmas that pit competing values against each other and to ask them to identify, articulate, and prioritize their own values in the course of discussing these dilemmas. You consistently urge students to respect each other's views and values, as you do. Students report home that you think everyone is entitled to his or her own values, leading to parental complaints that you are teaching moral relativism. How should you respond?*

Your educational strategy reflects what has usually been called *values clarification*, an approach that aims to get students thinking about values but avoids advocating or disparaging any particular values. Underlying such an approach is an admirable intent to avoid indoctrination, which demonstrates a praiseworthy commitment to the academic freedom of students.

The parental concerns are not without merit, however, and should be taken seriously. Values clarification curricula have indeed been based, in general, on the assumption that values are personal and arbitrary commitments that can sometimes be clarified but need never be reconsidered, revised, or replaced. In urging students to respect each other's views and values, and noting your own respect for all their values, you are suggesting to them that all values are equally good. What

I value may not be valued by you, and vice versa. We all have our own values, and who is to say whose values are better or worse? What is valued is relative to the person doing the evaluation.

This is all very well for some kinds of values. If I value chocolate ice cream and you value vanilla, I should indeed recognize that neither chocolate nor vanilla is inherently superior to the other. Which kind of ice cream an individual values is literally just a matter of taste. But what if I value racial equality, you value racial hierarchy, and our teacher urges us to respect each other's values? The implication here is that valuing racial justice is no different than valuing chocolate ice cream; it's simply what I happen to like, and others may legitimately have different tastes. The problem is that a general conception of values as relative leads, when we turn to moral values, to moral relativism. This is probably not what you intended to teach.

What, then, should you do? You should explain to the parents that you are trying not to indoctrinate their children in your own particular values but should acknowledge that, in your zeal to avoid indoctrination, you may indeed have conveyed a message of moral relativism that you did not intend. The solution is not to let the parents determine what and how you teach but to work with them in clarifying the problem and refining your approach to address their legitimate concerns.

What exactly is the problem? The problem is not that you have presented students with dilemmas that may have no clear resolution, nor is it that you have urged them to discuss such dilemmas without trying to impose your own responses, nor is it that you have urged that such discussions take place in an atmosphere of mutual respect. The problem is that in urging students to respect each other's views and values you have, perhaps unwittingly, conveyed the notion that all views and values are equally good. This suggests that there is no possibility of rational critique or reconsideration, which raises serious questions about the purpose and value of class discussion.

What you should do instead is to urge students to respect each other as persons, which includes respect for the right of each person to determine his or her own views and values. To say someone has a right to value whatever she values, however, is not to say that her values are correct or that they must not be criticized. It is perfectly legitimate for a student to try to convince another student to reconsider his or her values, and even legitimate for you, the teacher, to advocate or criticize particular values. What respect for others means is not that we agree with them but that our disagreements are pursued rationally, through efforts to convince—not through coercion or indoctrination.

Case 10–3 *As a teacher, you attempt to promote moral development by encouraging students to discuss moral dilemmas and to coordinate and reflect on the multiple viewpoints and justifications that arise in discussion. A parent thinks you spend far too much time on this and charges you with moral indoctrination. How should you respond?*

Moral indoctrination is not simply a matter of spending too much time on morality. Thus there are two distinct issues here: whether you are allocating classroom time appropriately and whether you are engaged in moral indoctrination.

Moral considerations are relevant in almost all areas of the curriculum at all levels of education. Provided you keep your focus on the topic you are supposed to be teaching, it is fully appropriate for you to raise relevant moral issues. If the parent is concerned that students in your math class are not learning math because you have them spend much of their time discussing the moral dilemmas of medical research, this is indeed a legitimate complaint. Students are in your class to learn math and this is what you should teach. If, on the other hand, the parent is concerned that students in your history class are spending too much time discussing the moral aspects of various historical events, this is less likely to be a legitimate complaint. History involves moral dilemmas of many sorts, and it is fully within the scope of your professional responsibility as a history teacher to encourage students to recognize and discuss such dilemmas.

Even where moral education is legitimate, moral indoctrination is not. In the present case, however, regardless of how much time you spend on the topic of morality, you do not appear to be indoctrinating your students. On the contrary, in emphasizing justification, reflection, and the coordination of multiple viewpoints, your approach recognizes the rational agency and moral autonomy of your students and is likely to promote the development of principled moral reasoning. In taking a moral development approach (rather than the values clarification approach of Case 10–2) you are not indoctrinating students in your own moral views and values, but neither are you conveying the message that whatever they happen to believe is neither better nor worse than what anyone else happens to believe. Instead you convey the message that, even in the case of complex moral dilemmas with no clear resolution, some responses may be better justified than others, and free discussion may lead us all to more advanced levels of moral understanding and reasoning.

Case 10–4   *State law or school policy requires you to begin each day by leading your students in reciting the pledge of allegiance to the U.S. flag. What if one of your students does not wish to participate in this? What if you don't wish to participate? What if the school insists that universal participation is fundamental to its program of civics education and its general commitment to citizenship as an aspect of character for all students?*

Individuals may object to the very notion of an official pledge of allegiance or to the idea of pledging allegiance to a flag. They may also object to the specific content of the official pledge, such as the claim that the United States is a nation "under God" or that it provides "liberty and justice for all." Whatever the objection, to require participation in the pledge of allegiance violates the principle that schools "may not impose or require belief or commitment" (Principle 1). Neither your students nor you should be required to pledge allegiance to the flag, to the republic for which it stands, or to anything else.

In public schools, as a matter of constitutional law, the right not to participate in a flag ceremony has been recognized since *West Virginia v. Barnette* (1943; see Chapter 2). Your students certainly have this right and should not be required to pledge their allegiance. If you don't wish to participate yourself, you may be required to make alternative arrangements for your students. If you cannot make alternative arrangements acceptable to the school you should probably consult a lawyer (or the ACLU) about your legal options and the potential consequences of various courses of action. Given your responsibilities as a teacher, your legal rights may be less clear in this case than those of your students.

If there is room for negotiation, you should note that respect for liberty is part of what it means to be a good citizen of a country that values liberty. As the Supreme Court understood in the middle of World War II, civics education will not suffer if students and teachers are free to decide for themselves whether to pledge allegiance to the flag. On the contrary, mandatory or mindless patriotism is antithetical to good citizenship.

And what if the result of all this freedom is that teachers teach about *Barnette* and students learn about their rights? Open discussion of these matters in class would do far more for civics education than a mandatory pledge.

Case 10–5 *Several of your students have been refusing to let a less popular child join their free time activities and some of them tease him relentlessly. What should you do?*

Children may have strong preferences concerning what they do in their free time and with whom they do it. They may have good reason to exclude a child who antagonizes them or does not play by the rules. The mere fact that a group of children did not want another child to join them is not necessarily reason to intervene. But if a particular child is regularly excluded from all free time activities, you may need to take some action on behalf of that child. Similarly, occasional teasing is a fact of social life and sometimes serves useful social purposes, but you have an obligation to see that no child is systematically targeted for harassment or bullying.

One way to address issues of this sort is to help other children see the effects of their behavior on the excluded or targeted child. This may elicit empathic feelings, which may change behavior and (in the long run) promote moral development.

If such efforts are not successful, however, you may have to set and enforce rules that enable all children to participate in free time activities and may have to punish students for teasing or otherwise targeting particular peers. More generally, it is often necessary to restrict and control student behavior in order to protect other students.

You should not assume, however, that such restrictions promote moral development. Morality is not a matter of doing what those in power require you to do. Behavior control is a necessity of social life but not necessarily a means of moral education. Moral reasoning and development flourish in an atmosphere of intellectual freedom.

Case 10–6 *Your students have been writing short stories and you receive one about a troubled student who goes on a murderous rampage. What should you do?*

In general, students should be free to express themselves in their stories. Censoring or punishing what they choose to express violates their right to freedom of expression (Principle 2) and their expectation of privacy in academic assignments (Principle 5b). Censorship and punishment also undermine the educational purpose of having them write stories.

In addition to your obligation to the academic freedom and education of your students, however, you also have an obligation to their personal welfare and the safety of other students. If you have reason to believe that a student has serious psychological problems that are not being addressed you should refer the student to a psychologist or counselor. If you have reason to believe that a student represents a physical threat to others, you must report what you know to an administrator or other appropriate authority. In deciding what to do, you can take into account what you know from any source, including the student's own writing.

There is reason to be cautious, however, about acting abruptly on the basis of creative writing alone. A general policy of reporting or punishing violent writing is unlikely to contribute to students' mental health or to school safety. The more likely result is that students will learn not to express what is really on their minds. Your response to student writing should take into account that violent thoughts are not uncommon and the opportunity to express and reflect on them in a fictional or academic context may help students deal with such thoughts effectively. In general, respect for student freedom of expression is good for mental health and a safer school environment. This does not mean you should ignore the content of student writing, but it should be a reminder that overreactions may do more harm than good.

Case 10-7 *You are a member of a governing board that is considering the role of character, values, and morality in the curriculum. Is this legitimate? What are your options? Does it matter whether the educational institution is public or private? Does the level of education matter? What if you are considering this as a member of a state legislature?*

The governing board of a school system is responsible for general matters of policy. Even if it has legal authority over the curriculum, such authority should be delegated to teachers and other experts in order to avoid indoctrination (Principle 4a). Thus it is within the legitimate authority of a governing board to determine that the school system for which it is responsible will address matters of character, values, and morality. Specific decisions—about how to conceptualize this, what exactly to teach, and how—should be left to schools, departments, curriculum committees, and individual teachers. Members of a governing board may have strong personal opinions, based in part on their political and religious ideologies, about what students should believe and value. They may also be subject to strong pressure from constituents who think they know just what should be taught and how. You should remind your governing board and constituents that, regardless of whether the topic is physics, history, character, or morality, curriculum "must be determined by teachers and other professionals on the basis of academic considerations" (Principle 4a).

These considerations apply regardless of whether a school is private or public and regardless of the level of education. Private schools, unlike public schools, are not subject to the First Amendment ban on government establishment of religion. Thus they are legally permitted to connect morality to religion and to advocate a mix of moral and religious views and values. They are also free, however, to recognize the role of intellectual freedom in education and to respect the academic freedom of teachers and students accordingly. Private schools are legally free to engage in religious advocacy, but they can and should avoid moral indoctrination.

The same considerations apply even more strongly to state legislatures, which are even more political and less expert on education than educational governing boards. Legislatures may have some legitimate responsibility with regard to the general purpose and equitable funding of public schools but should carefully restrain themselves from going beyond this.

Case 10–8 *You are a member of a college appeals committee that is hearing an appeal from a student who says he is being terminated from a teacher education program because he fails to meet a general requirement that all future teachers must have the proper dispositions to teach in our diverse, multicultural society and that this includes a commitment to social justice. The student being terminated says he believes in justice but sees social justice as a liberal concept inconsistent with his own conservative values. What information does the committee need to rule on this appeal?*

There are two considerations to be balanced here. On one hand, students and teachers, as people, have "an ultimate right to believe and value whatever they believe and value" (Principle 1). They may be exposed to alternatives, but may not be required to modify their beliefs or values. On the other hand, teachers "may be evaluated on the basis of the quality of their teaching" (Principle 1). It follows that students preparing to be teachers may be evaluated on their ability to teach, which includes their ability to work with a variety of students (see also Case 8–6).

It is thus important to clarify exactly why the student is being terminated. It is legitimate for a college of education to teach about social injustices and to provide student teaching experiences with a variety of students. If the teacher education student has been unable or unwilling to learn what he needs to know or has been unable or unwilling to work with certain kinds of students, this may be a legitimate reason for termination. If, on the other hand, these inabilities have simply been inferred from the student's attitudes, beliefs, or dispositions, the student should not be terminated. Whatever the student believes about social justice, he has a right to his beliefs.

Suppose, for example, the student believes that homosexuality is sinful and gay marriage is thus an abomination. Should this disqualify him from teaching? It might be argued that a student with such beliefs will be unfair to gay students, or at least less supportive than he should be, and is thus not fit to teach. This is an unjustified inference, however. Rather than terminate the student, it should be made clear to him that as a teacher he must be fair to all students, including gay students. Whether he can do this, consistent with his beliefs about homosexuality, is for him to decide. For college officials to determine that his religious beliefs will not permit respect and support for all his students is to make a theological judgment that they have neither the right nor the expertise to make. The role of the college is to teach him to teach and to evaluate his teaching.

There is, of course, the possibility that if the student is allowed to graduate he will be a biased teacher who favors students with views like his own and disfavors students who are gay or otherwise objectionable to him. But this is not the only possibility. It is also possible that he will recognize that he has been treated with respect—despite deep disagreement with his views—and that he will be committed to treating his own students that way. Of course we can't be sure of this outcome either. Unable to predict the future, our best option is to respect his academic freedom and teach him as best we can.

Case 10–9 *Your colleague is a passionate and popular teacher who always insists that she's teaching to change the world. She engages her students in activism and maintains that activism is not just volunteering. To be an activist, she insists, is to pursue a vision of social justice and cultural transformation. Should you be concerned?*

Your colleague's motivation and enthusiasm are commendable and likely contribute to the education of her students. Obviously you don't want to undermine this. Nevertheless, there is a potential for indoctrination in her approach that may be a basis for concern.

One consideration is relevance to the topic of the courses your colleague teaches. Course requirements, including requirements to engage in activism, should be consistent with the course title and description.

A related consideration is educational purpose. In an academic context, activism by students should contribute to their education. Of course genuine activism will also serve other purposes, and this may be critical to genuine commitment. But the activism should not be an end in itself. It should be related to other course material and part of an academic context of reflection and discussion that promotes understanding and learning.

A third consideration is freedom of choice. Students should be free to choose activist work consistent with their own beliefs and commitments, provided they meet legitimate academic requirements. Teachers should not regard or treat students as captive labor to serve their own political or religious purposes, however moral those purposes may be. In a political science course, for example, it may be useful and enlightening for students to participate in actual political campaigns, write about these experiences, and discuss them with each other, but they should be free to choose their candidates and causes.

Finally, there is a question of who defines social justice and determines what cultural transformations are needed. If students are drawn into seeing the world from a particular perspective without realizing there are other perspectives, this is indoctrination. If, on the other hand, they are encouraged to reflect on the complexities of justice and culture, they may develop their rational competencies with regard to moral reasoning and cultural critique and formulate justifiable moral visions of their own.

What if you conclude there are problems? Obviously you should be cautious in criticizing your colleague's teaching and especially cautious about accusing her of indoctrination. But colleagues have a responsibility to help each other maintain ethical standards. Your colleague probably agrees with you, in principle, that teachers should not indoctrinate their students, and probably does not see what she is doing as indoctrination. And maybe it isn't. But if you can draw her into a discussion of her teaching and help her see her class from her students' point of view, she may draw back from some of the gray areas that border on indoctrination. If it turns out she's resolutely over the line, of course, you may have to take stronger action.

Chapter 11
Ultimate Questions: Religion and Beyond

M any of the most intense controversies in education concern how educators address—or fail to address—ultimate questions of why we are here and how we should live our lives. Are these questions so special as to fall outside the bounds of academic freedom? Should principles of intellectual freedom be set aside when the issues at stake are fundamental ones that challenge our ultimate values, commitments, and identities?

On the contrary, the present principles of academic freedom recognize freedoms of belief and identity as central to intellectual freedom (Principle 1) and a necessary condition for meaningful freedoms of expression and discussion (see Chapter 4). The more fundamental the issue, the more crucial it is to respect the freedom of teachers to raise ultimate questions related to their topics and the right of students not to be indoctrinated in particular answers to those questions.

As a general matter of academic freedom, the principle of non-indoctrination does not forbid advocacy (Principle 4). The First Amendment requirement of governmental religious neutrality, however, forbids official religious advocacy in U.S. public schools, even where such advocacy falls short of indoctrination. Education about religion is legitimate and important in all schools, and religious indoctrination is a violation of academic freedom in any school, but questions of religious advocacy require us to distinguish public from private education and to make subtle judgments about a variety of practices and circumstances.

Case 11–1 During a literature class in a public institution, a student explains his interpretation of a character's actions with reference to sever-

al biblical stories, which he presents at some length. Another student complains that she's not here to learn religion. You're the teacher.

With regard to academic freedom, you must respect the right of the first student to express his views about whatever works you have assigned. The second student has a right not to be subject to religious indoctrination, but no such indoctrination appears to be taking place here.

With regard to the first student, interpretations are always based on prior knowledge. It is fully appropriate to interpret the actions of a character by making comparisons to other characters and other stories. In general, there is no academic reason to require or forbid reference to biblical stories, nor is there reason for you to favor or disfavor religious interpretations.

As for the second student, she can legitimately claim that she is in your class to learn about literature, not about religion, but it does not follow that she has a right not to hear or learn about religion in your class. Literature often touches on religious themes and is usually subject to religious interpretations of various sorts. Similarly, literature often raises issues of science or history and may be subject to scientific or historical criticism. It would be wrong for you to decide to teach about religion instead of teaching about literature, just as it would be wrong to focus your course on science or history instead of literature. Your students are taking your class to learn about literature and you have an obligation to make this the focus of the course. But you and your students may legitimately refer to religion, science, history, or anything else that enriches the discussion of literature. There is no obligation to avoid religion or any other topic. Provided religion comes up like any other topic and is freely discussed by those who deem it relevant, the discussion of religion does not constitute indoctrination.

Of course a problem could arise if religious perspectives came to dominate the discussion, either because so many students invoke such perspectives or because those that do go on at such length. As the teacher, you can keep the discussion moving and highlight alternative views. You can also remind students, as necessary, that the views of their fellow students are not necessarily the views of the school.

Aside from general principles of academic freedom, it is worth noting that the First Amendment specifically forbids the "establishment" of religion. This has often been interpreted as requiring a "separation of church and state," which in turn has led to a persisting constitutional myth that the U.S. Supreme Court has banned religion from public schools. In fact, there has never been any such ban. On the contrary, federal courts have always been clear that religious students have a right to freedom of belief and expression and that the public school curriculum may and should educate students about the various religions of the world and about the role of religion in history, culture, literature, and other areas of academic concern. Education about religion, as distinct from the inculcation of specific religious views and values, is fully consistent with both academic freedom and the First Amendment.

Case 11–2   *The student in Case 11–1 complains to you, as the responsible administrator, that her literature class has been turned into a Bible lesson and that her history class is taught from a Christian point of view. What should you do?*

At the level of principle, you can and should agree with the student that she has a right not to be indoctrinated in Christianity or any other religion. In fact, in any public institution, even advocacy that falls short of indoctrination would violate the First Amendment if it represents an official deviation from religious neutrality.

Whether either or both of these classes violate her rights, however, depends on exactly what is being taught and why. The mere fact that a student provides a biblical interpretation does not mean that the literature class is nothing but a Bible lesson. If, however, the teacher has organized the class around the Bible for religious reasons, or encourages religious comments while cutting off alternative reactions, the student has a legitimate complaint. Similarly, any legitimate history of the United States must take note of the influence of Christianity, and students must be free to provide their own perspectives. If, however, the teacher has organized the curriculum to highlight the beneficial influences of Christianity, the student's complaint may be justified and important—even if other students have no objection. As an administrator, your role is to see that curriculum is "determined by teachers and other professionals on the basis of academic considerations" (Principle 4a). Provided this is the case, there is unlikely to be a First Amendment problem even if there is mention of religion. If religious motivations are indeed driving the curriculum, however, you must protect the academic freedom and First Amendment rights of all students, even if most students and parents have no complaint.

These considerations of academic freedom apply regardless of whether a school is public or private. The present case (based on Case 11–1) involves a public school, but even a religious private school owes its students an academically justifiable curriculum in literature, history, science, and other fields. Religious private schools may of course advocate religious ideas. Advocacy is fully consistent with academic freedom provided it falls short of indoctrination (Principle 4). U.S. public schools, however, as a matter of First Amendment law, must maintain a stance of neutrality with respect to religion, which rules out official religious advocacy in public education.

Case 11–3 A "Committee of Concerned Parents and Citizens" presents you with a petition requesting that reverence be added to the official list of virtues of your school, which already has a list much like that of the school in Case 10–1. The petitioners say that reverence is the virtue that makes all the others meaningful. As the principal, how should you respond? Does it depend on the nature and purpose of the school? Does it depend on how much community support there is for the proposal?

Reverence may indeed be, for many, the virtue that makes all the others meaningful, and parents have a right to teach what they choose to their children. If you are the principal of a religious private school, you should keep in mind that many parents may be sending their children to your school, rather than a free public school, specifically because they want their children educated in an environment that endorses reverence. If there is substantial support for this proposal from the religious community responsible for the school, the addition of reverence to the official list of virtues may be appropriate. Even in this case, you should insist on decisions and policies consistent with principles of academic freedom. There should be a defensible process for determining the official list of virtues and changes to the list should be made in accord with that process. It is also possible and important for the school to advocate reverence without requiring that students hold or express any particular viewpoints.

If you are the principal of a public school, however, you must keep in mind that official religious advocacy violates the First Amendment even if it falls short of indoctrination. To see reverence as a virtue is not necessarily to favor any particular religion over any other but may be seen as favoring religion in general, which would violate the First Amendment requirement of religious neutrality. Thus reverence should not be among the list of official virtues, even if there is strong community support for adding it. But individual students are free to consider virtues other than the official ones, and there is no problem with teaching them that many people value reverence and other virtues not on the official list. Making the list a basis for reflection and discussion, in fact, may make it a legitimate component of moral education rather than an indoctrinative imposition on students.

Case 11–4 *The Committee of Concerned Parents and Citizens requests that all moral education curricula relying on peer discussion be discontinued because they teach children they can make up their own moralities, a view contrary to God's law. When you meet with them as the responsible administrator, members of the committee argue that this is just one facet of the larger problem that the school system is indoctrinating children in a secular humanist ideology. How should you respond?*

Peer discussion plays an important and positive role in learning, development, and education. It would be a profound infringement on academic freedom to ban it with reference to morality or any other topic. Nevertheless, there is a genuine danger that reliance on peer discussion of moral issues may convey to students the notion that whatever moral views they happen to hold are as good as those anyone else happens to hold. This relativistic notion of morality is not just contrary to what some may call "God's law" but also contrary to a variety of nonreligious views of morality as objective or at least rationally defensible. Even in a public school, moral discussion should be conducted in a context that conveys to students that, although they have a right to believe whatever they believe, this does not mean their beliefs are right. The purpose of discussion is not just to give students the opportunity to say what they think but also to give them the opportunity to hear what others think and to modify their views accordingly.

Reliance on discussion is consistent with the humanist notion that people are rational agents capable of profiting intellectually from free discussion. Religious humanists may see this capacity as a gift of God; secular humanists may see it as a basis for proceeding without reliance on God. But there is no need for a school to choose between these options, and the First Amendment requires that public schools avoid doing so. You can readily agree with parents that the school should not be indoctrinating students in secular humanism. But you should help them see that, even if secular humanists believe in human reason and freedom, commitment to reason and freedom does not constitute indoctrination in secular humanism.

Case 11–5   *Several students wish to register as an official student group and meet weekly after school to study the Bible and pray in one of several meeting rooms used by student groups in your public secondary school. The students also wish to post a notice on bulletin boards and to advertise their group in the student newspaper. As the administrator for student groups and related matters, you know that many students, parents, and members of your religiously diverse community will worry about the school becoming entangled with religion. What should you do?*

Happily for you, this issue has already been settled legally in a manner consistent with principles of academic freedom. The federal Equal Access Act, which applies to all public secondary schools, requires that if voluntary student groups unrelated to the curriculum are permitted to use school facilities, all such groups must be permitted on an equal basis. You must not favor or disfavor a student group simply because of the religious nature of their activities. You may, however, set general religiously neutral requirements for all groups, such as where and when they can meet, post notices, and so on. With regard to community reactions you should make sure everyone understands that the school is simply respecting the rights of all students on an equal basis and is neither favoring nor disfavoring religion in general or any particular religion.

The history of the Equal Access Act is interesting and revealing with regard to the interrelations of liberty, equality, and principled reasoning. In the early 1980s, with the strong support of the Reagan administration, Congress sought to reverse the Supreme Court decisions outlawing official school prayer. One possibility was a constitutional amendment exempting school prayer from the constraints of the First Amendment ban on the establishment of religion. Another option was to strip the federal courts of their power to hear school prayer cases. Unable to muster sufficient votes for either of these approaches, advocates of religion in public schools turned toward an alternative approach that protected student-initiated Bible clubs and other voluntary religious groups. Such an approach avoided the problem of official sponsorship of religion by school authorities but might still have violated the First Amendment establishment clause in favoring religious groups over other kinds of groups. The bill was therefore amended to protect freedom of association and expression for *all* student groups, including but not limited to religious groups. In its final version, the Equal Access Act requires that if a public secondary school permits student groups unrelated to the curriculum to meet on school premises, it must permit all such groups on an equal basis. This approach enabled the Equal Access Act to survive a First Amendment challenge because, rather than favoring religion, it simply treated private religious speech like any other private speech, consistent with First Amendment free speech decisions banning viewpoint discrimination.

The Equal Access Act has not just protected religious groups, however. To pass muster with the First Amendment, it had to protect all groups equally. As it turns out, perhaps unexpectedly but not surprisingly, the Equal Access Act has played a major role across the country in requiring school officials to permit gay-straight alliances and other gay-related groups to meet on school premises on the same basis as other student groups.

Case 11–6 *Your school requires that recognized student groups be open to all students on a nondiscriminatory basis, without regard to race, sex, religion, sexual orientation, or other such characteristics. A Christian group adopts a charter that limits its membership to Christians. What should be done?*

Your school's nondiscrimination requirement can perhaps be justified on the ground that no group is required to seek recognition as an official student group. Such recognition, it might be argued, should be sought and granted only in the case of groups open to all students. Students, like all persons, remain free to form and join groups with discriminatory membership requirements but they have no right to be recognized as an official student group if their group is not in fact open to all students. If students wish to form a chess club open only to whites or heterosexuals they are free to do so, but any chess club recognized by the school must be open to all students regardless of race or sexual orientation.

But what about religion? A chess club that bans Muslims is no less problematical than one that bans gays or African Americans. But a Christian club open only to Christians is not so clearly objectionable. A case might be made for maintaining a general requirement of nondiscrimination but exempting religious groups that wish to discriminate on religious grounds.

But what if African American students wish to form an African American student group open only to African Americans? What if the Young Democrats are leery of having Republican members, or vice versa? Allowing exemptions only for religious groups might be seen as unfairly privileging religious groups over others and, in a public school, might even be an unconstitutional preference for religion. A school might reasonably seek to avoid this problem by denying exemptions to any group. Students would remain free to form groups focused on matters of special concern to Christians, African Americans, Democrats, gays, or any other population—but for a group to be recognized as an official student group it would have to be open to all interested students regardless of religion, race, political affiliation, or sexual orientation.

In the case of a voluntary group, however, there is something slightly perverse about restricting its freedom to determine its own membership. Given such freedom, most student groups will probably choose to be open to all interested students. All students will thus be free to join most, if not all, groups. Although the school itself must be committed to nondiscrimination, a case can be made for eliminating nondiscrimination requirements for voluntary groups.

Another option fully consistent with academic freedom is to maintain a nondiscrimination requirement as the default option but allow any group to opt out by providing its own alternative membership requirements. This would encourage a policy of nondiscrimination but would also encourage reflection on that policy and would leave voluntary student groups free to make their own choices.

Case 11–7 *Your school has a long-standing tradition that the senior with the best academic record delivers a valedictory address at graduation. This year's valedictorian lets it be known that she is planning to thank Jesus for helping her get through school and will ask the audience to join her in prayer. As the responsible administrator, what should you do?*

Graduation ceremonies are perhaps more ceremonial than academic. Still, you should respect the intellectual freedom of the designated speaker. She is entitled to believe that Jesus helped get her through school and entitled to thank him for that. Whether she should ask the audience to join her in prayer, and whether you should permit this, is a more complex question that depends on the nature of the school and the legitimate expectations of the audience.

Suppose, in particular, that this is a public school. In that case, in addition to academic freedom considerations, there are issues of intellectual freedom associated with the First Amendment ban on government establishment of religion. If you chose a student to speak at graduation because you expected she would deliver a religious message, this would be an unconstitutional favoring of religion.

In the present case, however, the student was chosen on the basis of her academic record, not on religious grounds. She should be permitted to say what she thinks, regardless of the religious content of her message. To avoid misunderstanding, the graduation program should indicate how the valedictorian is chosen and be clear that her message is her own and is not necessarily endorsed by the school. If she believes Jesus helped her get through school and wants to thank him for this, so be it.

Asking the audience to join her in prayer, however, presents more of a problem. Even if no one is required to participate, some may feel compelled to do so and others may feel marginalized at their own graduation if they are among the few who choose not to participate in a prayer that does not represent their own views. This may be an outcome you wish to avoid; in a public school, it is an outcome you may be constitutionally required to avoid. You may discuss these matters with the student and try to convince her not to involve the audience. If she is intent on doing so, you will probably need legal advice. In a public school, this is not so much a matter of academic freedom as a conflict between the free speech and establishment clauses of the First Amendment.

Case 11–8   *Parents who wish to shield their child from evolution and sex education argue that what is being taught is contrary to their religious views. As the responsible administrator, what should you do?*

There are a variety of factors to consider here. You may wish to exempt the child from participation in some portions of some courses that their parents find religiously objectionable. Mere exposure to views contrary to one's religion, however, does not constitute indoctrination and does not violate any principles of academic freedom. You must protect the integrity of the curriculum by requiring students to earn whatever grades they receive by learning the essentials of any course, and you must protect the rights of students in cases where they are old enough to have educational preferences of their own.

There is no simple resolution to cases of this sort. You should aim for a creative solution that satisfies everyone and respects all of the rights and interests involved. If such a solution cannot be found you should seek input from all parties, get legal advice regarding your options, and make a decision consistent with academic freedom. Sometimes that's easier said than done.

Case 11–9 *The teacher of the Bible study course in your public high school talks about various miracles as if these were simply the questionable perceptions of various characters in the Bible rather than actual events in history. He also compares the Bible to the Koran and other religious texts as if they all had the same status, without acknowledging that the Bible, and only the Bible, is the true word of God. As a Christian student you are offended by this attitude and disappointed that the course is not what you expected. What should you do?*

Academic study is inherently critical, not a matter of faith. The study of the Bible in a public school is only legitimate if it is academic in this sense. You are of course entitled to believe the Bible is the word of God and entitled to believe in miracles. If you think your views are being censored or punished you should talk to the teacher and, if necessary, to an appropriate administrator. But if you are looking for a Bible course that takes a Christian perspective, you should recognize that no public school can constitutionally offer such a course.

Case 11–10 *Parents object to the availability in the public school library of Harry Potter books and others that promote witchcraft, as well as books about Muslim Americans and Islam. If the library collection cannot promote Christianity, they argue, then it should not promote paganism or Islam either. You're the librarian.*

You should agree with the parents that Christianity should not be disfavored in comparison with other religions. The mere presence of a book in the library, however, does not necessarily favor whatever viewpoints can be found in that book. Any good library collection will include books representing a variety of religious and other views.

You should redirect the focus of the parents to the collection as a whole and to the role of the library as a source of information and ideas.

Some parents may not be satisfied. Some may deem it reasonable to permit diverse conceptions of God, including Islamic conceptions, but not to include paganism or other challenges to monotheism. Others may accept Harry Potter but equate Islam with terrorism. You need not challenge their beliefs but must be unequivocal in defending the intellectual freedom of the library and its patrons against boundaries set on the basis of personal belief.

Case 11–11 *A student and her parents object to antireligious comments made by other students in your class. When you explain your support for academic freedom, they respond that academic freedom is itself a secular ideology and your support for it constitutes antireligious indoctrination. How should you respond?*

Insisting that even matters of religion are subject to principles of academic freedom may be seen as setting up academic freedom as the ultimate ideology that transcends all others. This may be deeply troubling to students or parents who see their own religious views as ultimate. Rather than insisting that academic freedom always trumps everything else, it would be better to note the variety of religious and other views held by students, parents, and faculty. Academic freedom can be seen as a pragmatic way of addressing the resulting controversies rather than as an ultimate ideology.

Even if academic freedom is something less than an ultimate ideology, however, it is more than just pragmatic. Its respect for all individuals, regardless of their beliefs, is a moral stance. This does not undermine the pragmatic argument for academic freedom, but rather supplements it with a conception of academic freedom as an educational ideal. Respect for intellectual freedom in academic contexts creates a moral community dedicated to learning and inquiry, with liberty and development for all.

Principles of Academic Freedom

1. *Freedom of Belief and Identity.* All persons, including students and teachers, have an ultimate right to believe and value whatever they believe and value, to maintain or change their beliefs and values as they choose, and to define themselves in terms of whatever beliefs and values they deem central to their identities. Educational institutions may present alternative views and values, but may not impose or require belief or commitment. Students may be evaluated and graded with regard to their understanding of and reasoning about curricular material but not on the basis of their agreement with particular viewpoints. Teachers and researchers may be evaluated on the basis of the quality of their teaching and research, but not on the basis of their viewpoints.

2. *Freedom of Expression and Discussion.* All persons have a right to express their views and to discuss them with others. In academic contexts, students and teachers have a right to express their views on any matter relevant to the curriculum even if those views are deemed to be false, absurd, offensive, or otherwise objectionable. Evaluations of student and faculty work, and restrictions on the time, place, or manner of expression, must be neutral with respect to viewpoint. Special steps to avoid misunderstandings may be necessary when an individual is speaking in an official capacity on behalf of an educational institution or professional organization or is addressing an audience that may fail to distinguish the individual from the institution, organization, or discipline that she or he appears to represent.

3. *Freedom of Inquiry.* Educational institutions should encourage students and faculty to pursue their own interests and ideas and should promote access to relevant sources of information. Inquiry

must not be suppressed by restricting access to particular authors, topics, or viewpoints, or by hindering the formulation of objectionable conclusions.

4. *Freedom from Indoctrination.* Educators and educational institutions must not require or coerce students to modify their beliefs or values. Efforts to convince students to modify their beliefs or values must be academically justifiable.

   4a. *Formulation of Curriculum.* Curriculum must be determined by teachers and other professionals on the basis of academic considerations. It is a responsibility of administrators and governing boards to explain and support justifiable curricular decisions and to educate their constituencies about the educational importance of an inclusive curriculum and the critical role of respect for academic freedom.

   4b. *Challenges to the Curriculum.* Suggested modifications of the curriculum should not be accepted merely to resolve a complaint, but neither should such suggestions automatically be rejected as illegitimate. In general, changes that expand the curriculum are more likely to be defensible than changes that contract or restrict it. On the other hand, additions may be illegitimate if what is added cannot be justified academically, and deletions may be appropriate if what is deleted was not academically justifiable.

5. *Equality, Privacy, and Due Process.* To the extent that violations of equal opportunity, privacy, and due process infringe on intellectual freedom in academic contexts, they are inconsistent with academic freedom.

   5a. *Equality.* All students and faculty have an equal right to academic freedom.

   5b. *Privacy.* Educators and educational institutions must refrain from academically unjustified inquiries into the beliefs, values, interests, affiliations, and expressive activities of current and potential students and faculty and from academically unjustified uses of information about individuals' beliefs, values, interests, affiliations, and expressive activities.

   5c. *Due Process.* Academic institutions must ensure that their formal and informal procedures provide sufficient due process to protect intellectual freedom.

Book Study

This is a book that lends itself readily to book study. Small groups of teachers, or others, can discuss cases relevant to their fields or concerns. I need hardly say more, but here are a few (increasingly ambitious) suggestions:

1. Arrange for a group of teachers to meet, perhaps once, or perhaps on a regular basis, to discuss cases chosen from Chapters 5–11. Make up and discuss variations relevant to your own circumstances.

2. Invite students, parents, administrators, or others to join the discussion. Academic freedom, as defined in this book, is not a special right of teachers, much less a secret ritual to be shielded from outsiders. Academic freedom is intellectual freedom in educational and research contexts. Even if disagreements arise—and even if they are not resolved—discussions of academic freedom should incorporate the multiple perspectives of those with differing roles in the educational system.

3. Develop a statement or policy on intellectual or academic freedom for your department, school, or professional group. The five principles of *Liberty and Learning* could be a starting point for discussions leading, perhaps after one or more rounds of revision, to formal adoption. Even a policy that is not binding on anyone may serve a useful purpose in providing ethical guidelines, or at least a starting point for discussion, regarding the roles, rights, and responsibilities of students, teachers, parents, and administrators in a system of academic freedom.

4. Form a statewide academic freedom coalition (unless you live in Nebraska, in which case contact AFCON). Organizations likely to be interested include:

state and local teacher organizations;

the state library association;

the state ACLU affiliate;

faculty senates;

state and local units of the American Association of University Professors;

literary, scholarly, and press organizations;

and others, perhaps unique to your state.

For information about the Academic Freedom Coalition of Nebraska, see www.afconebr.org.

References and Suggested Readings

Chapter 1

On intellectual freedom in elementary and secondary education, see

Gloria Pipkin and ReLeah C. Lent, *At the Schoolhouse Gate: Lessons in Intellectual Freedom* (Portsmouth, NH: Heinemann, 2002);

ReLeah C. Lent and Gloria Pipkin (Eds.), *Silent No More: Voices of Courage in American Schools* (Portsmouth, NH: Heinemann, 2003);

Jean E. Brown (Ed.), *Preserving Intellectual Freedom: Fighting Censorship in Our Schools* (Urbana, IL: National Council of Teachers of English, 1994);

Diane Ravitch, *The Language Police: How Pressure Groups Restrict What Students Learn* (New York: Vintage, 2004).

See also the website of the Five Freedoms Project (www.fivefreedoms.org).

On intellectual freedom in higher education, see

John K. Wilson, *Patriotic Correctness: Academic Freedom and Its Enemies* (Boulder, CO: Paradigm, 2008);

Alan C. Kors and Harvey A. Silverglate, *The Shadow University: The Betrayal of Liberty on America's Campuses* (New York: Free Press, 1998).

See also the website of the Foundation for Individual Rights in Education (www.thefire.org).

On the role of intellectual freedom in learning and development, see

David Moshman, *Adolescent Psychological Development: Rationality, Morality, and Identity, 2nd edition* (Mahwah, NJ: Erlbaum, 2005).

On teacher authority and autonomy in elementary and secondary education, see

Chris W. Gallagher, *Reclaiming Assessment: A Better Alternative to the Accountability Agenda* (Portsmouth, NH: Heinemann, 2007).

On teacher authority and autonomy in higher education, see

Matthew W. Finkin and Robert C. Post, *For the Common Good: Principles of American Academic Freedom* (New Haven, CT: Yale University Press, 2009).

See also the AAUP 1940 Statement of Principles on Academic Freedom and Tenure. This classic statement is available in American Association of University Professors, *Policy Documents and Reports, 10th edition* (Baltimore: Johns Hopkins University Press, 2006) and on the AAUP website (www.aaup.org/AAUP/pubsres/policydocs/contents/1940statement.htm).

On student rights in elementary and secondary education, see

David Moshman, *Children, Education, and the First Amendment* (Lincoln: University of Nebraska Press, 1989).

See also the National Education Association's Code of Ethics of the Education Profession (www.nea.org/aboutnea/code.html) and the website of the Five Freedoms Project (www.fivefreedoms.org).

On student rights in higher education, see

Alan C. Kors and Harvey A. Silverglate, *The Shadow University: The Betrayal of Liberty on America's Campuses* (New York: Free Press, 1998).

See also the websites of the Foundation for Individual Rights in Education (www.thefire.org) and the American Association of University Professors (www.aaup.org).

On community autonomy, see

Chris W. Gallagher, *Reclaiming Assessment: A Better Alternative to the Accountability Agenda* (Portsmouth, NH: Heinemann, 2007).

Chapter 2

Cases cited: Meyer v. Nebraska, 262 U.S. 390 (1923); Pierce v. Society of Sisters, 268 U.S. 510 (1925); Minersville School District v. Gobitis, 310 U.S. 586 (1940); West Virginia State Board of Education v. Barnette, 319 U.S. 624 (1943); Adler v. Board of Education, 342 U.S. 485 (1952); Sweezy v. New Hampshire, 354 U.S. 234 (1957); Keyishian v. Board of Regents of the University of the State of New York, 385 U.S. 589 (1967).

Chapter 3

Cases cited: Tinker v. Des Moines Independent Community School District, 393 U.S. 503 (1969); Board of Education, Island Trees Union Free School District No. 26 v. Pico, 457 U.S. 853 (1982); Bethel School District No. 403 v. Fraser, 478 U.S. 675 (1986); Hazelwood School District v. Kuhlmeier, 484 U.S. 260 (1988); Bishop v. Aronov, 926 F.2d 1066 (11th Cir. 1991); Morse v. Frederick, 551 U.S. 393 (2007).

Post-Hazelwood cases denying First Amendment protection in curricular contexts include Boring v. Buncombe County Board of Education, 136 F.3d 364 (4th Cir. 1998) (secondary education); Lacks v. Ferguson Reorganized Sch. Dist. R-2, 147 F.3d 718 (8th Cir. 1998) (secondary education); Bishop v. Aronov, 926 F.2d 1066 (11th Cir. 1991) (higher education); Hosty v. Carter, 412 F.3d 731 (7th Cir. 2005) (higher education).

Post-Hazelwood cases recognizing First Amendment protection outside the curriculum include Good News Club v. Milford Central School, 533 U.S. 98 (2001) (elementary education); Saxe v. State College Area School District, 240 F.3d 200 (3rd Cir. 2001) (secondary education); Rosenberger v. Rector and Visitors of the University of Virginia, 515 U.S. 819 (1995) (higher education); DeJohn v. Temple University, 537 F.3d 301 (3rd Cir. 2008) (higher education).

Chapter 4

On the development of rationality and identity, and the role of intellectual freedom in learning and development, see

David Moshman, *Adolescent Psychological Development: Rationality, Morality, and Identity, 2nd edition* (Mahwah, NJ: Erlbaum, 2005).

The first paragraph of the quote from the American Library Association concerning freedom of inquiry is from the *Library Bill of*

Rights and the second paragraph is from *Access to Resources and Services in the School Library Media Program: An Interpretation of the Library Bill of Rights.* These and related documents are available on the American Library Association website (www.ala.org).

For principles and policies concerning intellectual freedom in higher education, see the website of the American Association of University Professors (www.aaup.org).

For principles and policies concerning intellectual freedom at all levels of education, see the website of the Academic Freedom Coalition of Nebraska (www.afconebr.org).

Chapter 5

For an impassioned defense of the literary canon, see

John M. Ellis, *Literature Lost: Social Agendas and the Corruption of the Humanities* (New Haven, CT: Yale University Press, 1997).

Chapter 6

Cases cited: Epperson v. Arkansas, 393 U.S. 97 (1968); Edwards v. Aguillard, 482 U.S. 578 (1987); Kitzmiller v. Dover Area School District, 400 F. Supp. 2d 707 (M.D. Pa. 2005).

For a history of antievolutionism, see

Ronald L. Numbers, *The Creationists: From Scientific Creationism to Intelligent Design* (Cambridge, MA: Harvard University Press, 2007).

For a critical analysis of antievolutionism, see

Robert T. Pennock, *Tower of Babel: The Evidence Against the New Creationism* (Cambridge, MA: MIT Press, 1999).

Chapter 7

On the history and politics of history education, see

Gary B. Nash, Charlotte Crabtree, and Ross E. Dunn, *History on Trial: Culture Wars and the Teaching of the Past* (New York: Vintage, 2000);

Linda Symcox, *Whose History? The Struggle for National Standards in American Classrooms* (New York: Teachers College Press, 2002).

For critiques of history education, see

James W. Loewen, *Lies My Teacher Told Me: Everything Your American History Textbook Got Wrong* (New York: Touchstone, 1996);

Bill Bigelow and Bob Peterson (Eds.), *Rethinking Columbus: The Next 500 Years, 2nd edition* (Milwaukee, WI: Rethinking Schools, 1998).

For an alternative history of the United States, see

Howard Zinn, *A People's History of the United States* (New York: Harper & Row, 1980).

On patriotism in elementary and secondary education, see

Joel Westheimer (Ed.), *Pledging Allegiance: The Politics of Patriotism in America's Schools* (New York: Teachers College Press, 2007).

On patriotism in higher education, see

John K. Wilson, *Patriotic Correctness: Academic Freedom and Its Enemies* (Boulder, CO: Paradigm, 2008).

On the construction of knowledge (Case 7–6), see

David Moshman, *Adolescent Psychological Development: Rationality, Morality, and Identity, 2nd edition* (Mahwah, NJ: Erlbaum, 2005).

Chapter 8

Tom Lehrer's live rendition of "National Brotherhood Week" can be found on his album, *That Was the Year That Was* (Burbank, CA: Reprise Records, 1965).

On "political correctness" in elementary and secondary education, see

Diane Ravitch, *The Language Police: How Pressure Groups Restrict What Students Learn* (New York: Vintage, 2004).

On "political correctness" in higher education, see

Alan C. Kors and Harvey A. Silverglate, *The Shadow University: The Betrayal of Liberty on America's Campuses* (New York: Free Press, 1998).

On the role of intellectual freedom in learning and development (Case 8–3), see

David Moshman, *Adolescent Psychological Development: Rationality, Morality, and Identity, 2nd edition* (Mahwah, NJ: Erlbaum, 2005).

Chapter 9

For a detailed policy concerning sexuality and academic freedom, see the Academic Freedom Coalition of Nebraska website (www.afcone-br.org).

The quotes in the introduction are from J. M. Coetzee, *Giving Offense: Essays on Censorship* (Chicago: University of Chicago Press, 1996).

On adolescent competence (Case 9–2), see

David Moshman, *Adolescent Psychological Development: Rationality, Morality, and Identity, 2nd edition* (Mahwah, NJ: Erlbaum, 2005).

Cases cited in Case 9–4: Tinker v. Des Moines Independent Community School District, 393 U.S. 503 (1969); Bethel School District No. 403 v. Fraser, 478 U.S. 675 (1986); Hazelwood School District v. Kuhlmeier, 484 U.S. 260 (1988).

The Hechinger quote in Case 9–4 is from Fred M. Hechinger, "Political shift on 'vulgar' speech," *The New York Times*, July 15, 1986, pp. 17, 20.

On library policy (Case 9–5), see policies of the American Library Association at www.ala.org.

For excellent books on sexuality and censorship in relation to children and education, see

Marjorie Heins, *Not in Front of the Children: "Indecency," Censorship, and the Innocence of Youth* (New York: Hill and Wang, 2001);

Kristin Luker, *When Sex Goes to School* (New York: Norton, 2006);

Janice M. Irvine, *Talk About Sex: The Battles over Sex Education in the United States* (Berkeley: University of California Press, 2002);

Jeffrey P. Moran, *Teaching Sex: The Shaping of Adolescence in the 20th Century* (Cambridge, MA: Harvard University Press, 2000);

Judith Levine, *Harmful to Minors: The Perils of Protecting Children from Sex* (New York: Thunder's Mouth Press, 2003).

Chapter 10

On moral development, see

John C. Gibbs, *Moral Development and Reality: Beyond the Theories of Kohlberg and Hoffman, 2nd edition* (Boston: Allyn & Bacon, 2010);

David Moshman, *Adolescent Psychological Development: Rationality, Morality, and Identity, 2nd edition* (Mahwah, NJ: Erlbaum, 2005).

On moral education, see

Larry Nucci, *Nice Is Not Enough: Facilitating Moral Development* (Upper Saddle River, NJ: Merrill Prentice Hall, 2009);

Stephen Law, *The War for Children's Minds* (London: Routledge, 2006);

B. Edward McClellan, *Moral Education in America: Schools and the Shaping of Character from Colonial Times to the Present* (New York: Teachers College Press, 1999).

For an example of social justice education, see

Jessica Singer, *Stirring Up Justice: Writing and Reading to Change the World* (Portsmouth, NH: Heinemann, 2006).

Chapter 11

For an overview of religion in public schools, see

Joan DelFattore, *The Fourth R: Conflicts over Religion in America's Public Schools* (New Haven, CT: Yale University Press, 2004).

Key Supreme Court decisions on religion in public education include: McCollum v. Board of Education, 333 U.S. 203 (1948); Zorach v. Clauson, 343 U.S. 306 (1952); Engel v. Vitale, 370 U.S. 421 (1962); School District of Abington v. Schempp, 374 U.S. 203 (1963); Stone v. Graham, 449 U.S. 39 (1980); Wallace v. Jaffree, 472 U.S. 38 (1985); Lee v. Weisman, 505 U.S. 577 (1992); Santa Fe Independent School District v. Doe, 530 U.S. 290 (2000).

On the role of peer interaction in learning, development, and education (Case 11–4), see

David Moshman, *Adolescent Psychological Development: Rationality, Morality, and Identity, 2nd edition* (Mahwah, NJ: Erlbaum, 2005).

The U.S. Supreme Court upheld the constitutionality of the Equal Access Act (Case 11–5) in Board of Education of the Westside Community Schools v. Mergens, 496 U.S. 226 (1990).

Index

abstinence curricula, 118–119
academic freedom, xiii, 3–14, 142
  as First Amendment right, 16,
    23–29, 42–45
  as intellectual freedom, xiii, 11–13,
    46–55
  intrinsic to education and research,
    13–14, 45
  principles, viii–ix, xiii–xiv, 16,
    46–55, 143–144
  right of students, 3, 7–8
Academic Freedom Coalition of
  Nebraska, xiv, 146
Adler v. Board of Education, 23–24,
  27, 29
administrators, 3, 12, 92–95, 99–100,
  106, 117, 134–141
  role protecting academic freedom,
    12, 52–53, 64–65, 77–78
adolescents, 4, 9, 117
  rationality of, 111
advocacy, 8, 11, 51–53, 132, 135
African Americans, 96–98, 107, 138
Alaska, 40
Alito, Samuel, 40–41
American Association of University
  Professors, xiii–xiv, 8, 16, 146
American Civil Liberties Union,
  xiii–xiv, 125, 146
American Library Association, 50–51
anti-Semitism, 87

Arkansas, 72
armbands, 14, 30–31

balanced treatment, 72–73, 81
Barnette. See West Virginia v.
  Barnette
Bethel v. Fraser, 33–35, 41, 113–115
Bill of Rights, U.S., 16, 20, 43–44
biology, 72–85
Bishop v. Aronov, 39
Black History Month, 96–97
Black, Hugo, 22–24, 43
Blackmun, Harry, 35, 39
Board of Education v. Pico, 32–33, 39
Bong Hits 4 Jesus, 14, 40–41
book selection, 59–71, 89
Brennan, William, 24, 27–29, 35–39,
  43
Breyer, Stephen, 40–41
bullying, 126
Burger, Warren, 114

canons, 59–68
Caravaglia, Jody, 111
Catholic schools, 17
censorship, vii, 30–41, 59–70,
  115–116
character, 120–122, 127–128
Chelsea, Massachusetts, 112
children, 4, 8–9, 50–51, 108, 126
Christianity, 17, 72–73, 134, 141

Christians, 73–75, 78–79, 103–106, 138–139
"City to a Young Girl, The," 111–112
civics education, 125–126
civility, 33, 105, 114
Clinton, Bill, 117
Coetzee, J. M., 108–109
communism, 13, 22–29
community control of education, 3, 9–11, 65–66, 135–136
Constitution, U.S., 15, 70
construction of knowledge, 4, 46, 51, 75, 94–96, 136
Cooke, Sam, 86
creationism, 72–85
cultural transformation, 70, 131
curriculum
  academic basis for, 5, 52–54
  biology, 72–85
  challenges to, 53–54
  faculty responsibility for, 6, 52–53, 119
  history, 86–92, 95–97
  literature, 59–71
  school authority over, 14, 32–40
  sexuality, 118–119

Dartmouth, 24
democracy, 4, 6, 10–11, 20–21, 44, 46–47, 52, 82, 95–96
Des Moines, Iowa, 30
development, 7, 51, 124–126, 136, 142
diversity, 21, 61–62, 104–105, 137
Douglas, William O., 22–24
drugs, 14, 40–41
due process, 54–55

Eckhardt, Christopher, 30
education, 120
  as inculcation, 43
  as rational process, 19, 46

elementary, 4, 6, 11, 29, 115–116, 126
higher, 4, 11, 16, 25–26, 29
intellectual freedom in, xiii–xiv, 13, 46, 107
private, 9–10, 17
public, 4, 10–11, 46–47
secondary, 4, 6, 11, 29, 111, 137–138
vs. indoctrination, 3, 46, 70–71, 130–131
Edwards v. Aguillard, 73, 81
Elders, Jocelyn, 117
elementary education, 4, 6, 11, 29, 115–116, 126
Epperson v. Arkansas, 72, 81
Equal Access Act, 137–138
equality, 54, 138–139
evaluation and grading, 47–49, 74
evolution, 72–85
Exodus, 18

faculty autonomy, 5–6
Feinberg Law, 23–24, 27–29
First Amendment, xiii, 13–45, 17, 107, 112
  ban on indoctrination, 16–22
  basis for academic freedom, 23–29, 42–45
  establishment of religion, 72–73, 133–134, 137–138, 140
  free exercise of religion, 19, 22
  free speech and press, 13–45, 111
First Freedom, The, 111
flag salute, 13, 17–22, 125–126
Fortas, Abe, 30
Fourteenth Amendment, 15–17
Frankfurter, Felix, 26, 43
Fraser, Matthew, 113–115
Frederick, Joseph, 40–41
freedom
  academic (see academic freedom)

from indoctrination, 7–8, 10–11,
    16–22, 51–54
of association, 138–139
of belief, 7–8, 47–48, 107
of discussion, 48–49
of expression, 30–32, 48–50
of identity, 7–8, 47–48
of inquiry, 50–51
to learn, 7–8
to teach, 5, 8

gays, 100–107, 115–116, 129, 138
genocide, 87–91
geology, 74, 82
Germans, 16
Ginsburg, Ruth Bader, 40–41
Gobitis, Lillian and William, 18
governing boards, 3, 12, 78–82, 92,
    119, 127–128
    role protecting academic freedom,
    12, 52–53, 66–68
Gypsies, 87–88

harassment, 55, 102, 104–106, 118,
    126
sexual, 114, 117–118
Harlan, John Marshall II, 26
Hazelwood v. Kuhlmeier, 14, 16,
    32–40, 42–44, 116
Hechinger, Fred, 114
Hentoff, Nat, 111
higher education, 4, 11, 16, 25–26,
    29
hiring decisions, 27, 55, 106–107
history, 86–97, 106
Holocaust, 87–90
human rights, 48, 70, 100–103
humanism, 136–137

identity, 7–8, 47–48, 73, 106, 132
ideology, 4, 7–8, 10, 47–48, 73,
    136–137, 142

Indians (Native Americans), 88–91
individual accommodations, 54,
    78–80, 109–110, 140–141
indoctrination, 16–22, 51–54, 61–63,
    86, 122–125, 130–131, 142
antidemocratic, 4, 10–11, 17,
    20–21, 44, 46–47
distinct from education, 3, 70–71,
    75
nature of, 7–8, 51–54, 124
violation of student rights, 3, 5,
    7–8, 70–71, 75, 132
institutional autonomy, 4–5, 26–27
instructional methods, 93–95
intellectual freedom, 11–13, 21–29,
    46–55
    basis for learning and inquiry, 4,
    6–8, 46, 101, 107
intelligent design, 73, 84–85
intolerance, 98–107
Islam, 141–142
Island Trees, New York, 32
Israel, 87–88

Jackson, Robert, 13, 19–22, 43–44
Jehovah's Witnesses, 17–19
Jews, 87–88
Juneau–Douglas High School, 40

Kennedy, Anthony, 40–41
Keyishian v. Board of Regents, 13,
    27–30, 40, 42, 44
King, Martin Luther, Jr., 96–97
Kitzmiller v. Dover, 73
Ku Klux Klan, 17
Kuhlmeier, Cathy, 33

learning
    as rational process, 7, 19, 46, 51,
    136
    requires intellectual freedom, 4,
    6–8, 13, 46, 51

legislatures, 3, 67, 82, 95–96,
118–119
Lehrer, Tom, 98
liberty. *See* freedom
literature, 59–71, 132–135
local control of education, 11, 43,
65–66
Louisiana, 73

Marshall, Thurgood, 35
masturbation, 117
Mexico, 98
Meyer v. Nebraska, 16–17, 43
Minersville v. Gobitis, 18, 43
Missouri, 33
moral relativism, 122–123, 136
morality, 3, 7, 13, 46, 101, 120–131,
136
Morse v. Frederick, 14, 40–41
Mount Rushmore, 84–85
multicultural societies, 10, 20–21, 47,
128–129
multiculturalism, 61, 66–67
Muslims, 138, 141

National Education Association, 7
Native Americans (Indians), 88–91
Nebraska, xiii–xiv, 16–17, 99–100,
117–118, 146
neutrality, 10
political, 21–22, 35
religious, 22, 132, 135, 137–138
viewpoint, 38–40, 47–50, 52,
101–102, 138
New Hampshire, 24–26
New York State, 13, 23–24, 27–29
New York Times, 114

obscenity, 108, 111–112
offensiveness, 41, 48–49, 54, 102,
104–107, 109, 114–115, 118
Oregon, 17

paganism, 141–142
parental authority, 3, 8–9, 16–17,
62–63, 74–75, 110–113
Parks, Rosa, 96–97
patriotism, 18–21, 86, 92, 125
peer discussion, 102, 136–137
Pennsylvania, 18
Pierce v. Society of Sisters, 17
pledge of allegiance, 13, 18–22,
125–126
political correctness, 98
pornography, 109–110
privacy, 54–55
public education, 4, 6, 10–11, 13–14,
18–47, 52

rationality, 7, 19, 48, 51, 124–125,
130, 136–137
relativism, moral, 122–123, 136
religion, 3–4, 9–11, 132–142
in public schools, 18, 22, 72–85,
133–134
research, 5–6, 12, 50–51
reverence, 135–136
Roberts, John, 40

Saint Augustine, 108
Scalia, Antonin, 40
school boards. *See* governing boards
school libraries, 32, 51, 111–113,
115–116, 141–142
school newspapers, 14, 33–39, 116
schools, 4–5, 10–11, 13–14, 17
science, nature of, 83–85
scientific theory, 82–85
Scopes, John, 72
secondary education, 4, 6, 11, 29,
111, 137–138
secular humanism, 136–137
selection of books, 59–71, 89
separation of church and state, 133
sexual harassment, 114, 117–118

sexual orientation, 100–107,
    115–116, 129, 138
sexuality, 33, 108–119
Smart, Leslie, 33
social justice, 70–71, 128–131
Souter, David, 40–41
South Africa, 26
Spectrum, 33
State University of New York in
    Buffalo, 27
Stevens, John Paul, 40–41, 114
Stone, Harlan Fiske, 18
students, 59–62, 73–74, 90–91,
    96–97, 141
    rights of, 3, 6–9, 12–22, 30–41,
    46–55, 110–111, 113–115,
    128–129
subversives, 23–29, 55
Supreme Court, U.S., 13–45, 125,
    134
Sweezy v. New Hampshire, 24–27,
    29, 40, 42

teachers, 12, 22–29, 63–64, 68–71,
    82–92, 95–96, 98–106, 109–110,
    120–127, 130–134
    authority over curriculum, 5–6,
    51–53, 76–77
    role protecting students, 51–53,
    82–83, 133

Tennessee, 72
tenure, 5, 53, 100
Thomas, Clarence, 40–41
Tinker v. Des Moines, 14, 30–44, 114
Tippett, Leanne, 33
tolerance, 98–107, 120–121

United Nations Genocide
    Convention, 87
Universal Declaration of Human
    Rights, 70
University of Nebraska–Lincoln,
    xiii–xiv, 99–100, 117–118
University of New Hampshire, 25–26

values, 120, 122–124, 127–128
Vietnam, 14, 30
viewpoint discrimination, 38–41,
    47–50, 52, 101–102, 138
violence, 68–70, 91–92, 126–127

Warren, Earl, 24–26
Washington State, 113–114
West Virginia v. Barnette, 13, 16,
    18–22, 30, 36, 39–40, 42–44,
    125
White, Byron, 34–35
World War II, 22, 87, 125